# FOR THE YOUNG

*By the same author*

—

TO FEED THE HUNGRY
THE OUTLAWS OF PARTINICO
WASTE
A NEW WORLD IN THE MAKING

DANILO DOLCI

# FOR THE YOUNG

—

*Translated from the Italian by*
ANTONIA COWAN

MACGIBBON & KEE

Note: The stories in this book have been
adapted from material collected between
1954 and 1966, first published in full in

BANDITI A PARTINICO (1955)

INCHIESTRA A PALERMO (1956)

SPRECO (1960)

and

CHI GIOCA SOLO (1966)

# CONTENTS

# PREFACE

I WILL make my introduction as short as possible, since I remember how when I was young I used automatically to skip a long preface at the beginning of a book.

Your letters come to me from all over the world. From Northern Italy, for instance, Grazia writes: 'We hope you will not be sent to prison. We will be thinking of you on the day of the trial.' From Mario and Sergio: 'We're doing all we can to help you, we're being very good, and praying for you.' From Mariassunta: 'I want you to be set free,' and from Maria Teresa: 'Let's hope you'll be freed.'

A number of young people write to me from Switzerland, and from Scandinavia, to tell me how they have organised meetings among their friends to discuss the problem of the poorer countries, and how they have started projects to promote practical help. Others write to our Centre to ask if we think that when they have finished their studies they might be usefully employed here.

From London comes this letter: 'Our class has made up a play of your life story. I was in the play and I was supposed to be your wife Vincenzina and David Sandland played the part of you. We would like you to come to our school and see the play whilst you are in London. We would all dress properly. When we first did it to the school in morning assembly we did not dress up. Yours sincerely, Angela Argyridou.'

Many of the young people I meet on my travels greet me as an old friend, and I am always very sorry when I cannot stay and talk to them for as long as I would like. We get a number of letters asking for 'more detailed information about people in Western Sicily'. Others are keen to know more about our own views. And many others write just to send us 'best wishes for the future'. Micky sends from New York a drawing of a flower; some Russian girls send a piece of cross-stitch embroidery; and from South America come post-cards of parrots, pile-dwellings, skyscrapers, and the monstrous fungoid growths of shacks of the *favellas*.

All these letters, all these questions, are so full of hope and fresh enthusiasm—how am I to answer them all as fully as they deserve? Up till now I had always tried to reassure myself by arguing that the work itself, the work to create a new world, was the best answer. But I was never quite convinced; and eventually I began to think to myself: 'What if I were to write to them—not just the usual little note, but a real, serious letter, a letter that could be made into a book for them all to read?'

These letters of yours give me a great deal of pleasure, but also, I must admit, they worry me a little. Why should they be addressed to me? Could it be because people think me better than I really am? And what can I tell them that will be new?

In the end I made up my mind. 'The important thing is,' I told myself, 'that I should write to all of them, as well as I am able. I shouldn't bother so much with trying to think up something new to say, but, rather, I should try and put down a few of the things that I think are true, things that have been tested and proved by the experience of some of the people I most respect: things that I myself would have found it useful to have been told when *I* was young.'

The characters you are going to meet in this book are all real, living people: I know each one of them personally. It is to them that I have entrusted the task of telling you (for they can do it better than I could)—telling you directly, in their own words, what it is really like in Sicily, and what absurd lives too many people still have to lead.

This book-letter, then, is clearly not meant as entertainment. The material is rough, harsh, often crude: just a few voices from among those of the hundreds and hundreds of millions of people in the world who could tell you the same story—offered to you, with your still uncalloused sensibilities, as a subject for reflection; and as a demonstration of faith in your capacity for new revolution, which older people too often seem to have lost.

# FOR THE YOUNG

# For the young

DEAR FRIENDS,

The more experience we have of life, and the more we reflect on our experience, the clearer it becomes to us that one of the most fundamental and universal human problems is *waste*. Too often, the sort of conditions that people are forced to live in mean that they are not even aware of the difference between waste and the proper use of resources. Of course people cannot be expected always to recognise the value of things which are still unfamiliar to them: but all too often they fail to make proper use of the resources already at their command. And if, as is often the case, they are incapable even of turning their own natural gifts to account, it is hardly surprising that they fail to recognise possibilities of improving the world around them.

One day, I suggested to a small group of children that we might perhaps try out a new game, a serious game: 'Let's go for a number of walks together, each one of us being particularly watchful and observant, and then let's try writing down every observation and discovery made, and every question that occurs to you.' We discussed where we should go, and eventually decided on one walk by the sea and one in the countryside, and one up into the mountains by day and one by night. The children were Daniela, aged five; Chiara, aged seven; Amico and Ruggero, aged nine; Cielo, aged eleven; Libera, aged twelve; and Bruna, fifteen.[1]

Here are a few of the discoveries and a few of the questions that came out of our expedition to the seaside, picked from among others rather less coherent and to the point.

*Daniela*   Why does the sun move?
　　　　　Where does the sea start?

---

[1] The girls' names end with 'a', the boys' with 'o'.

*Chiara*    If you put your foot down on wet sand, it goes dry; then when you lift your foot up again, the wet comes back.

Why is it that soles swim flat in the water and other fish swim upright?

How was the sand made?

How are shells born?

Why are little children so fond of the sea?

*Amico*    If rough things are under water, like sand when it's wet, they stick to each other much more than when they're dry.

Water is pale itself, but it makes everything it touches turn darker.

Why does water cool down and warm up more slowly than land?

*Ruggero*    How do fish manage to hear each other, and communicate?

How do fishes' gills work?

*Cielo*    You can see hundreds of different shapes in the foam on the waves—hearts, and horses, and all sorts of things.

Why is the sea salty?

How many thousands of years might a family of fish last?

Why can you see better under water with goggles than you can with the naked eye?

Why is it that sometimes when you half shut your eyes you see lots of little rainbow-coloured circles?

*Libera*    Usually in the morning, before the wind gets up, the sea looks more transparent. Then when the little waves begin to come, the sand rises up from the bottom like lines of little clouds, and that makes the water all murky. But after each wave the sand settles and the water is clear again, till the next wave comes along. When the wave comes up over that bit where those sandy hillocks are, it stirs up the little clouds of sand; then as it washes back again the sand spreads out and sinks and disappears, and the water is clear again.

The water looks paler where the sun is on it.

The further away you look, the bluer the sea is.

The sea always looks quite calm and flat on the horizon.

*Bruna*  How can water, which is so soft itself, shape things as hard as rock? Even a little stone has taken ages and ages to weather—you see in its shape the mark of thousands of years.

From a distance, the sea looks quite uniform: but if you see it from close to, you realise every wave is different, every one has its own particular shape and colour, and its own different way of rolling up and breaking on the beach.

These children are not prodigies, they are just ordinary children. But because their minds have not yet been made dull and stale (and also, of course, because being young and green they are less aware of difficulties), they have a zest and appetite for life which enables them to look at things both with a sense of wonder and, at the same time, with a cool and penetrating curiosity, and makes them more open to new experience than someone who is already trapped in a set way of life.

Once a person is alert and responsive enough to be able to ask himself an intelligent question, he is already well on the way to finding the answer.

If someone objects, at this point, that it was only the presence of an adult that stimulated these particular children on this occasion, then that only underlines my point: it is essential that adults should share activities with children in a way that will enable them, as naturally as possible, to stimulate the children's interests.

For just as children's interest and curiosity can be stimulated by an environment where observation and enquiry are constantly encouraged, so their minds can be blunted and dulled, their development nipped in the bud, where the attitude of people around them is one of not caring, of preoccupation with trivial things, of shirking thought and rejecting outright whatever is unfamiliar and not immediately understood; or, worse, where the environment is a veritable abyss of hunger, disease and misery—as it still is over vast stretches of the world.

Even for well-meaning people, it is all too easy to stunt the growth of the young: there are hundreds of millions of children in the world whose potentialities are allowed to go to waste.

Another day, we spent several hours walking in the countryside. Many of the questions that occur to the children in fact range back over thousands of millions of years.

*Daniela*   Every stone makes a different noise.
      Why do flowers smell?
      Where do butterflies come from?

*Chiara*   What makes roots have different shapes?
      Why are blackberries black and almonds brown?

*Amico*   Up in the mountains, and down by the sea, you can hear sounds much more clearly.
      If you pull a piece of straw, it doesn't break; but if you bend it, it does.
      The butterfly has a sort of jumping, fluttering flight. Every butterfly, and every insect and every bird, flies a different way.
      If you look in a mule's eyes you can see the reflection of everything around, but it's all distorted. You can see reflections in a person's eyes, too, but in a mule's eyes they're better.

*Ruggero*   Some stalks are solid, but others are hollow—like bamboos, for instance.
      How do olives manage to stand up to drought for so long?
      Why is it that when a lizard gets its tail broken, it can grow a new one, but we can't grow new bits?

*Cielo*   Every flower smells different.
      Many kinds of plants live in communities.

Where did the first seed come from?

How does every fruit have a different taste?

Why do some plants have leaves growing upwards, while others have leaves that hang down? And there are also some plants whose leaves start off by growing upwards, and then curve down again—like the leaves of bamboos.

How do bamboos manage to be so flexible, and yet so hard?

How on earth do some animals come to be camouflaged with protective colouring—like lizards among the grass, or some sorts of snakes; or soles, which you can't see against the sand? And some fish even have it both sides: from underneath, they look the same colour as the surface of the sea, or the sky, and from above they're invisible against the sea bed.

*Libera* Look at this dead thistle—a spider's been weaving its webs all among the prickles. The thread is very very fine, yet the webs are quite dense. These little black specks must be the remains of gnats which the spider has sucked. It's cunning of the spider not to stay in the web—perhaps he wants to keep out of danger himself, too: but he tries to keep out of sight so as not to frighten the insects he wants to eat, so they'll be more likely to come into the web. The gnat doesn't see the spider, which would look like a huge monster to him: all he sees are these beautiful threads shimmering like strings of diamonds, and flashing rainbow colours in the sun. Spider's webs are like those pretty advertisements you see on the television. And the Mafia, and some of the politicians, are like spiders!

*Bruna* If grass is pulled up, it withers: in order to stay alive, it has to have its roots in the earth to suck up nourishment.

It takes root much more easily if you transplant it when it's green.

When the grass first comes up, it's all quite green. It's

only later that it dries up. People should think of ways to prevent it from drying up, because once it's withered it's not much use to anyone.

None of us, children or adults, can develop properly unless we are allowed opportunities like this for concentration and creative thinking; and unless we establish a new attitude towards each other, and towards the world itself. It is only too easy for the process of natural curiosity and learning through direct experience to be obstructed, instead of being encouraged and developed as it should be. And so, as a person grows up, his understanding of the world comes to be based on a vast mass of unconnected acts of faith, concerning both trivial and fundamental questions, all jumbled up in his mind with little fragments of his own experience. It is not surprising then, if after a while he begins to take it for granted that he is quite incapable of ever co-ordinating his vision of life into an organic whole.

Too many people, as they grow up, allow their attention and their interests to be limited and restricted to an insane degree. Nowadays, the number of people who still have a direct and basic relationship with the real world is getting smaller and smaller: the artist, perhaps, and the scientist, and the peasant, and the fisherman—but how open and free is even *their* relationship?

It is a hard task to change people's attitudes and make reform possible. The future has so much to offer mankind—yet just think how much leprosy there still is in the world, how much poverty, how many castes, how much uncompromising hostility, how much insane and pointless murder of every kind.

Another day, we went for a walk in the mountains.

*Daniela*   If you put a bit of marjoram in your mouth and chew it, it stings your tongue.
Why does marjoram smell like this?

How do small branches come to grow out of the big branches?

How do birds fly?

*Chiara*    Why are some flowers all the same colour, while others have two colours, or even more?

How was the mountain made?

Birds' feathers are hollow inside. Some of them have a tiny hole at the end. Perhaps why they're hollow is to make the bird's wings lighter so that it can fly better.

Why don't we have wings so we can fly too?

*Amico*    If you look down from the top of a tree, you can see the mist better.

Some trees are quite hairy.

Pine-needles are round when they're green, but when they dry up they split in two, and one side is rounded and the other side is hollow like a split cane.

The tufts up the sides of some feathers are all stuck together. If you poke them with your finger, up to a certain point they stay all in one piece, but then if you poke a little harder they suddenly split apart.

*Ruggero*    A ladybird has white spots on its head—the two little white spots near the front must be its eyes. It has six little legs, and a pair of antennae with tiny blobs on the end. It has one red pair of wings with litte black dots on, and underneath those there's a pair of transparent wings. I think the outer wings must be to keep out the cold—they're quite hard—and also to protect it from other things. The ladybird is shaped rather like a tortoise. On the under side it's all black and stripey, and it has a bit of dark brown on its throat.

If you make the ladybird walk on a very thin twig— on a pine-needle, for instance—it hangs upside-down. When you get it to walk along upside-down on your arm without falling off, it hangs on to your skin, you can feel it sort of tickling; and then when you want to pick it up it holds on to the hairs on your arm—it tries

B

to cling on, because it doesn't want to go. Some lady-birds are much keener to fly away, though.

If you turn a ladybird over on to its back on your hand, it can turn itself the right way up again; but if you put it on its back on a flat stone, it can't turn over. For a while it keeps waving its little legs very fast, trying to turn over; but then sooner or later it gives up, and bunches all its legs together on to its chest, and lies quite still.

Sometimes if you put it on a stone and it wants to turn round and face the other way but finds it can't because it can't get a grip with its feet, it'll suddenly flash its wings open and jump round.

*Cielo*      All the stones you find in one part of the mountain are the same colour, and made of the same stuff: but by the sea, the stones you find on one stretch of the beach are all different colours.

How does moss ever manage to live on stones?

If you crush a piece of marjoram and twist it in your fingers, it smells much stronger. If you put the flower up to your nose, it makes you sneeze.

Why do ladybirds exist?

*Libera*     The shell of a snail isn't just light and strong: often it's a perfectly beautiful shape too. From one small point, it goes spiralling out and out, and the opening has a most beautiful curve, whatever angle you look at it from. And the different colours are lovely, too.

Sometimes snails fasten themselves on to long thin blades of grass, and for protection they make them-selves a transparent veil, like a bit of glass, which is also attached to the grass-blade.

*Bruna*      When you're in a wood and you can't see the sun itself any more, it looks as if it's the trees that are shining. The old trunks are rough and flaky, and the young ones are all firm and smooth, and there's a transparent gum oozing out of the cracks. The trees turn incredible colours—gold, and flame colour, and brick-red, and grey. In the silence you seem to hear the voice of the mountain; and every tiny sound—a little pebble moving, or the crackle of dry twigs, or the call of a bird that you can't see—every sound seems so much clearer.

Here are a few of the reflections made by the children at this point:

*Amico*   If a person stays always in the same place, he thinks everywhere else is like that too, he thinks the whole world is just the same, and so he gets bored. If you see the same old things all the time, you don't like them any more—you stop noticing them, even. But when you go to new places, you notice all sorts of different things.

It's like what happens with the scent of marjoram, for instance: at first you smell it very strongly, even from a distance, but when you're near it for any length of time you gradually get used to it and so it seems to smell less and less.

*Ruggero*  When you've been looking at a ladybird for some time, you think you know everything about it: but afterwards if you look again you keep noticing new things.

*Cielo*   It's one thing to see mountains on a map, but quite a different thing actually walking over them.

To really get to know about trees, I'd have to actually climb them.

When you're really happy yourself, then you feel more like being nice to other people.

The children's experiences lead them gradually towards making more systematic observations, and they begin to feel the need for a new, direct relationship with the environment.

Being young means essentially, I think, being capable of growth, being capable of living in a creative symbiosis with other people and with the environment: and, obviously, this is not simply a matter of being young in years.

On the magnificent beach of the Bay of Castellammare (which is usually deserted, since the people do not easily overcome their ancient fear of the sea) a woman is lighting a little fire down near the edge of the water, and laying out on a grill a row of freshly-caught red mullet, while her family play about in the sea and sun. A number of youths—some of whom are, in fact, qualified teachers—happen to be hanging around nearby, and they start muttering: 'Really! What a disgrace! What a way to behave! How can anyone still do things like that? *Decent* people would go to a restaurant . . .' and so on, making fun of her, their voices getting louder and louder . . . And yet these same young men apparently see nothing immoral in continuing to serve as touts at election time for a local candidate who is notoriously well disposed towards the Mafia, in the hope that he will pull strings for them in return and get them fixed up with jobs.

However young in years one may be, narrow-mindedness and fear and the inability to think for oneself can make one old in every other sense.

The August evening grows darker and darker, and soon four stars appear in the sky. We are high up on the mountainside above Montelepre. Amico is happiest of all because we are going to write with his new pen tonight. (It has a little light so that you can write in the dark with it: it was a present from his aunt.)

*Daniela*   I like the morning better than the evening, because in the morning I can start playing, but in the evening when it gets dark I'm frightened if I'm left alone.

*Chiara*    I only like the night when the moon and stars are out, because the moon gives a bit of light, and the stars shine. The mountain turns quite black at night. What a lot of stars! How did the stars get there?
            Why is it that when we walk along, the moon and the stars seem to move along with us?

*Amico* At night when I switch off the bathroom light, as soon as I'm in the dark I think there are bogey-men coming after me, so I run as fast as I can back to where there's a light on, either to Mamma or to you, to kiss you goodnight.

People are more frightened at night because in the dark you can come on danger suddenly, whereas by day you can see ahead and so you have time to save yourself.

If you look down from the mountain, the further off the lights of the villages are, the more they seem to twinkle; and the nearer they are, the steadier they shine.

With all those stars floating in the sky, why do some of them fall down?

Why should I be on this planet?

Why aren't I a horse?

*Ruggero* We can't see each other in the dark, but some animals can see us.

How ever did there come to be so many stars in the sky?

*Cielo* As night falls, the mountains grow darker and darker, and the lights shine brighter and brighter.

When you look at the lights of a town from far away, why is it that you seem to see rays of light spreading out round each one?

How was the sky made?

Why should *I* have been born into the world? And why should *you* be my father, and Mamma my mother? (Not that I'm complaining!)

Is it possible that this earth is the only place where there are people, and living things?

Why can't we live for ever, instead of having to die?

Stars are huge, of course—they're far, far bigger than us, and they last far longer: but they haven't got brains like we have.

The whole world's one great mass of things to find

out about; and then we look away from our planet and there are millions more questions to ask till we learn all about space.

*Libera*    A village, or a town, looks much prettier from away up here at night: the sky is so vast that the lights seem to have a kind of diamond brilliance they wouldn't have ordinarily.

*Bruna*    At night on the mountainside, it's as if you're suspended in the darkness, and people seem tiny. How does everything exist?

When I was a little boy, I was fascinated by the stars. My mother used to take me to church, and when the little bell rang for the Sanctus and I knelt down along with all the others, the most perfect moment for me was when I shut my eyes tight and saw millions of bright stars spinning in the blackness of space, and pictured myself as a tiny speck of goodness in the great universe.

In one of the first books on cosmogony that I read, it was stated that astronomers had already discovered four thousand galaxies, each one consisting of about one hundred thousand million stars. But that was some time ago: nowadays, we read even in popular illustrated magazines that they have established the existence of many millions of galaxies, and that the earth is at least five thousand million years old.

I am sure Amico has not yet begun browsing among books on astronomy, but a few weeks ago he asked me: 'Why is it only over the last two thousand years that men have agreed to calculate time in the same way?' And after I had taken Chiara up into the cupola of Saint Peter's some months ago, and she was talking to the others about it, she referred to it as 'Saint Peter's capsule'. However difficult or impossible it may be for people to shake off prejudice and broaden their minds by their own efforts, a certain degree of enlightenment comes willy nilly as new instruments and new lines of research reveal to us more and more clearly the true nature of the world. New instruments, new techniques and experiments contribute, directly or indirectly, towards a new, comprehensive and coherent picture of the world that not so very long ago would have been inconceivable, and give us the possibility, in the widest sense, of cultivating the earth. And these new insights cannot but be of profound significance also in the social field.

One day, I read to the little group a statement made by an economist in a book brought out very recently, in several languages, by a number of well known publishers: 'Military expenditure can help towards maintaining a high level of employment, production, and consumption in advanced economies that might otherwise be threatened by depression.' I re-read this, explaining some of the terms used, then asked them for their opinions on it.

*Cielo*    Instead of manufacturing arms, they could give the people some other sort of work.

*Ruggero*  Yes, I'd say they shouldn't make guns and things for killing people—they should change to another job.
           That book is wrong, because other sorts of work are far more important—like producing food for people to eat, or building houses to shelter people from cold. There shouldn't be weapons.

*Amico*    It's not a sensible thing to say. Why should a man work at something that is going to kill other people? Instead of wasting money on killing, they should do good things—things that would be useful to everyone.

*Chiara*   Yes, I agree, what he says is wrong. I think someone who thinks a thing like that must be very ignorant.

*Amico*    Making weapons isn't a proper job, any more than killing people is.

*Cielo*    Weapons are worse than useless, they're harmful and dangerous.

*Ruggero*  The bosses of the weapons factories are ignorant too, and so are the men who order them to be made, because they don't realise that once these weapons exist they may be killed themselves. And the workers who work in the arms factories are ignorant too, they just don't understand.

| | |
|---|---|
| *Cielo* | Besides, even though it seems an advanced economy, it can't really be if it's based on arms. |
| *Amico* | It's like a disease. |
| *Bruna* | Exactly. The bosses are ignorant, the workers are ignorant—and so is the man who wrote that: he can't have thought about what war means—he can't have thought about people dying. |
| *Libera* | Yes, from what he says I'm sure he can't have thought it out properly. |

Printed matter is, for the most part, a purveyor of ready made, pre-packed culture. Even though (like traditions, schools, radio and television, and so on) it may perform a useful function as a transmitter and a stimulus, not only does it often prevent us from achieving a fuller, simpler, and more direct communication with the world, but also (as anyone who is in the least concerned about this knows very well) it can quite easily become an instrument for manipulating people, whether intentionally or unintentionally, in such a way that they are made to act against their own interests and stand in the way of their own progress.

As the rate of new discoveries and new achievements gets faster and faster, the new generations trying to learn how to profit from the experience and the mistakes of their forerunners will be faced with an ever increasing problem of how to assimilate critically what has gone before.

Most people's imaginative capacities are limited: too many people pass much of their lives as unresisting prisoners of the most automatic conditioned reflexes. The average individual's imaginative capacities tend for the most part, even in the face of new possibilities and new opportunities, to be stifled by the old mechanical reactions. Things which are at first hailed by a few as harbingers of a new life gradually come to be worshipped more and more by people in general only as they come more and more to represent the old life.

And so it happens that even today we leave some of the greatest responsibilities in the world to certain white-collared troglodytes who, instead of being armed with catapults for throwing stones, are now armed with jets for dropping H-bombs.

We allow piles of facts and jumbles of information to accumulate in our minds, and unconsciously we try to steer our way between them, instead of absorbing and assimilating them into an integrated personality. We accept more or less passively the old pattern of 'exploit or be exploited', and only take opportunities for co-operative action when they are thrust upon us, instead of creating and organising for ourselves the new groups we need, and teaching ourselves to achieve growth and progress through collaboration with others. And in the same way our relationship to society in general falls into the same old stereotyped patterns. We need to change all this, and create a society in which there is at the same time more diversity, and more co-ordination: a society at the same time simpler, and more complex—in other words, a more organic type of society. Obviously when we focus our attention on something that is new and strange to us, it will seem at first very difficult to grasp. But not impossible, as long as we know how to approach the unfamiliar in a way that will make it more manageable.

I picked another sentence from the same book and put it to the little group, simplifying and explaining it as I read:

'Acquaintance with a higher standard of living creates an awareness of the necessity for further development, but at the same time makes the attainment of a higher standard more difficult.'

*Ruggero*   Yes, for instance if a Negro comes from Africa and sees how the whites do certain things, if they're living in a civilised way, he can learn from them, and so he'll be able to do things better himself.

*Amico*   And if white men go to Africa, they can learn things they're not so good at from the Negroes. If someone sees other people doing things better than he can, or living a better life—well, he'll probably learn from them.

*Cielo*   People should try on their own, too. But if they see others doing things better, that'll stimulate them into trying to do better themselves.

*Chiara*   When my little brothers are better than me, then that makes me want to be good too.

*Daniela*   If I see that Chiara's got a new dress, and I haven't, then I start wanting one too. If Mamma buys Chiara a dress, I want her to buy me one too.

*Ruggero*   But I'd like you to read the second part of that sentence again, because I've just thought of something.

*Danilo*   'Acquaintance with a higher standard of living . . .' he says . . . 'makes the attainment of a higher standard more difficult.'

*Ruggero*   But that's not true.

*Cielo*   No, it's not true. Because if a person decides he wants to do something new, he may make mistakes and not succeed at first, but if he's patient . . .

*Amico*   Where there's a will there's a way.

*Cielo*   Yes. Suppose there are two people, for instance, who have to draw water up from a well all through the summer. If one of them is cleverer, sooner or later he'll get hold of a donkey and tie a rope to it and make it do all the pulling so that he doesn't have to work so hard. Well, when the other man sees this, he'll want to do the same; and if he hasn't got a donkey he'll try to think of some other way to save himself having to work so hard.

*Amico*   When Daniela went and put her arms round you a short while ago, that made Chiara want to go to you as well!

*Ruggero*   If the babies in a village are always dying, people think it's just fate. But if another family comes to live there and none of *their* babies die, at first the villagers are just rather envious, but soon they start trying to find ways to stop their own babies dying—they want to learn how to keep *their* children alive too.

*Amico*    And suppose there is an island somewhere, all belonging to one landowner, and he has peasants working for him, and they are poor, and can't get their children enough to eat because the owner exploits them and keeps everything for himself. Well, those men will get together and organise a revolution—not to harm the owner, but just so that they can be people too. They'll take over the land, and work it together for themselves; and they'll use all the gold bracelets and the diamonds from the necklaces to buy tractors. And the man who used to be the owner will be made to work too!

*Danilo*    Perhaps what the writer means by the second part of his sentence is that if someone sees other people living well and spending a lot of money, that may just make him want to spend a lot of money too, rather than encouraging him to produce more.

*Libera*    Well, I agree with the first part of his sentence, but not the second, though I can't really say why not.

*Bruna*    Me too. If people really decide they want to improve things, they may not succeed at once, they may make mistakes at first—they may even find themselves going backwards for a bit: but all the same, sooner or later they're bound to get into the right gear for going forwards and making real progress.

One of the most fundamental and essential revolutions to which our age is committed is the change-over from authoritarian methods of running society (with power concentrated in the hands of relatively few strong men—generals, priests, bosses and landowners, judges, police, the paterfamilias, and so on), to the more healthy system of common progress through participation by everyone.

To create a better world, we *must all* make our contribution. It is safer to have responsibility shared; better to be able to draw on the experience of many than to have everything entrusted to a privileged few. Basically it is in the interests of everyone to co-operate, and only by learning to co-operate for the good of all (even though this will no doubt mean going through periods of conflict and difficulty) can men ever hope to live in harmony and make real progress. And, besides, it is only by taking part in common action that a man can develop fully as an individual.

In protesting against the inadequacies of the old order of things, young people too often tend just to cut themselves off. But their rejection of what is out of date and useless should not be merely an indulgence in vague feelings, or a withdrawal into a kind of cultural apartness: their rebellion, their anger, ought to be canalised and directed into the creation of a new society, a new way of life. They must be firm in their refusal to collaborate in what they feel to be wrong, and persistent in their practical attempts to realise their ideal world; they must not betray their finest dreams in selling out to the highest bidder, they must not allow themselves to be bought in the name of 'realism' by whoever has the money to 'set them up'. Valid alternatives cannot be realised without valid personalities, without new minds and a new productive capacity.

Of course, we must also realise that educating ourselves to live by means of open groups and new forms of planning—in other words, educating ourselves for a new world—will take a lot of determination, and a lot of time. But it is absurd meanwhile just to leave everything to those in power, to sit and wait for governments to act; it is absurd to rely solely on political solutions: genuine changes, genuine reforms, can only be brought about by the commitment of single people and groups of people with new ideas.

Our society is so full of conflict and corruption that it is clearly necessary for us to find a new sort of cure before it becomes any more diseased. What we need is a group of specialists who can collaborate in their diagnosis and prescription for the various ills of society, basing their recommendations not on old laws and old dogmas but on a new, scientific analysis of the economic, biological and psychological factors. And, clearly, society can remain fundamentally sound only if there is healthy interaction and collaboration among its various groups and members.

Being civilised means, I think, being able to recognise that one's own good and the common good are one and the same thing, and being able to pursue one's own interest in the common interest, within a world-wide perspective and taking a long term view. Faced with the continual discovery and development of new sources of energy (and historians of science and technology tell us that even today each of us—on average of course—now has at his command energy many thousands of times greater than a few centuries ago), and with new possibilities opening out before us all the time, are we to give up any attempt to find a way of organising the world rationally according to our genuine and basic needs? No: just as certain diseases that once used to kill off whole populations have today been practically eliminated from the world, so now a new commitment could cure mankind of other ills—poverty, war, the oppression of the weak by the strong, and so on—which up till now have always seemed incurable and inevitable. Chronic pessimism, like chronic optimism, is just a naïve way of not facing reality. Once we give way to our fear of knowledge and our fear of life, we have already begun to die.

Now I will let my friends take over.

# Vincenzo, a young man in prison

THREE nights ago, I had a dream about pigs. And cows too —they were browsing among clumps of grass. I always dream about cows, and mountains, and goats, and sheep, and lambs —every night. All my life I've looked after animals, and I'm always thinking about them. Last night I dreamt I was out in the countryside where I used to take the animals, and along came a man, and then I saw he was my father. He was leading a ewe with two lambs, and the ewe was suckling one of the lambs and the cow was suckling the other. Then another old man came along and killed this lamb of mine. And then he caught sight of our hen who was squatting down laying an egg, and he started to break the eggs and suck them and throw away the shells.

And then he ran off, and I chased him for a bit meaning to give him a thrashing with my stick. But then my mother appeared, and she said: 'Who broke these eggs? And who killed the lamb?' (It was the old man who'd killed the lamb— he was a horrible old man.) Then my father said: 'Well, we may as well cook the lamb now and eat it.' But I said we should throw it away under an olive tree because it was too small. So he chucked it under the olive, and we left it there.

I also dreamt about some people who were taking pigs in a lorry to sell at the fair, and they'd put little leather collars round the pigs' necks.

I had another dream last night, too. I dreamt I was up in the mountains, and I was taking a herd of cows to drink—about three hundred of them. There were other cows, too, all over the hillside. But there wasn't any water, and there I was searching all over the place for water. Ever since I've been shut up in this horrible prison I've been dreaming about animals and fields and mountains and things.

30

I dreamt about my uncles, too, last night. They said to me: 'Come on, bear up, you mustn't be such a coward!' And then I dreamt I saw a nail in the wall outside a door, and there was a chain hooked onto the nail, and at the other end of this chain, just inside the door, there was a pig attached. The pig trotted out and started squealing, but I couldn't think what it wanted. There was water there, but it didn't want water. Then this man came out and asked me: 'Well, did you get the broccoli leaves?' 'Yes,' I said. Then I start walking along beside him, and after a bit he says: 'Aren't you going now?' 'No, I'm not going yet,' I told him. 'You haven't paid me for the last few days' work, and I'm not going till you've paid me.' Then he gave in, and handed me a thousand lire. 'But this isn't enough,' I said. You see, he thought three hundred lire a day was too much—he didn't want to pay me more than two hundred. 'You can take this thousand lire, or nothing,' he said, and in the end I took it and went away.

Once, I dreamt—(what month is it now? February? It was in February last year)—I dreamt I was galloping along the sea shore on a horse, with a machine-gun in my hand, when I saw two bulls goring each other with their horns. Then the very next day the man came with my summons (that wasn't a dream, though: the bulls on the sea shore were what I dreamt), and I was put in the cells and punished because the police sergeant had called me 'bardascio' and I'd called him 'bardascio' back. I don't know what bardascio means, but it must be a bad word. Then the priest came to see me (that wasn't a dream either!) and he told me if anyone called me bardascio I shouldn't answer. So I asked him: 'Why shouldn't I answer back?' 'Because you don't understand,' he says. But if someone punches you, shouldn't you punch him back?

I always dream about animals—animals roaming free out in the fields—because I've always looked after animals, ever since I was five years old. I was born among the animals.

I was the first to be born, then my brothers and sisters started coming along after me. When I was about five I began looking after the animals. They weren't our animals, though: my father

was hired by the year (how many months in a year?) or by the
half year. Or else they gave him four or five thousand lire a
month. I don't know how many months there are in a year.
I don't know if I'm seventeen or nineteen. We could get someone to write home and ask them to look at the birth certificate.
I can count up to fifty, but I don't understand money because
I've lived all my life out in the countryside. I never went into
the village, and I never saw another human being, except my
father every now and again. My mother doesn't understand
money either, and she can't even count. I used to cook herbs
and roots and wild cabbages, and eat them. I can tell a fifty lire
piece, but that's all, and I can't add them up with other money.

If you can't get any work, you eat wild greenstuff and herbs.
Hunger will drive a man to anything. Sometimes you can't even
see out of your eyes. Some people kill themselves—people do
terrible things out of hunger. But if only you've got work,
you've got everything. If a man's paid a decent wage, he'll do
his work properly, and learn to mix with other people, and be
able to talk to them without quarrelling. But when there's no
work—I tell you, we just go about killing each other. If a man
knows how to set about getting a job, and how to make a good
impression, then the boss will take him on and trust him. But
someone like me—who would ever trust me? I'm always getting
into fights with people, and then I go wild and don't realise
what I'm doing. For instance, suppose another man had some
bread, or some money, and you and me pinched it off him—
what would we do to make sure he didn't talk? We'd kill him.

Once I broke my arm falling off a horse—it was my boss's
horse, and I was taking it to water. But even though my arm
was broken, I never got any of the money I should have had as
compensation.

Sometimes there would be as many as six of us lads together
out in the fields, and not one of us knowing how to count
money. Usually, though, I was out on my own. And all the
time these filthy rich just go swaggering up and down town
in their smart boots!

Each of us in here—we're each of us booked for prison, like

we're all booked for the graveyard: we all come to it in the end. We quarrel, and fight, and kill each other, and end up either here in prison or else in the graveyard. And when a man is let out of prison, he isn't reformed, you know: he goes out more of a savage than when he came in. He'll go and seek out his enemy, and say to him: 'You've stained my honour—and now you're going to pay for it!' and he kills him. And unless there are spies around, he'll get away with it. For instance, take the three of us here: if another bloke had harmed one of us, and we killed him, then unless someone squealed no one would know anything about it. But the authorities are always putting their bloody spies on us. If it wasn't for the spies, crimes would be committed right under their noses and they wouldn't be any the wiser.

I used to be away from the village for six months or a year at a time, and when I went back I was so wild looking that the children didn't recognise me—they threw sticks and stones at me till I ran away. Once one of them flung a handful of little bits of paper, carnival confetti, over me, and I caught him and bit his finger.

I've got one brother of thirteen, and another of twelve, and neither of them can count, or deal with money. Then there's a little brother of five, and a sister of six. The other two died. And there's also another sister younger than me, but I've no idea how old she is—twelve maybe, or sixteen, I don't know. She's gone and got married since I've been here in prison.

When I was very young, the police came round one day and took us all off to the barracks. We were all crying. They took my mother, and all of us children. They didn't catch my father till later, though—he jumped off the cart and escaped. They put my mother in prison, with the baby she was nursing, and sent the rest of us children away again. They kept my mother in for six months, then when they caught my father they let her out.

After that, I went and stayed out in the countryside and looked after the animals. I used to sleep in the straw. I didn't get undressed at all, I just burrowed into the straw with all my clothes on. I didn't have any blankets or anything. Often I had bare feet, and there were times when I had nothing at all to eat. I was always crawling with lice—covered with them. My boss wouldn't let me drink the cows' milk—if I did, he used to beat me with a stick. In the morning I had bread and curds, and in the evening bread and onions, or bread and olives when there were olives. Every now and again the boss would come round and see me. Sometimes I used to leave the animals and come down from the mountain to where there were some houses. I'd go up to a house, and all the dogs would start barking—but I'd brave it out and go up to the door and beg for a bit of bread because I was so hungry. Some people would give me a bit, others wouldn't give me any. But sometimes I got as much as I wanted, and even enough to take away with me. Other times, though, I had to steal it.

One day, I was walking back to the village hand in hand with my father when all of a sudden he spotted the police, and at once he rushed off, and I was left standing there by myself. The police started shooting at him, but he dived into the river. Some of them were on horses, and some were on foot. They had great big guns, as big as this—'Ninety-ones—and they shot him in the back: if it had been just a bit higher or just a bit lower, he would have been killed. Then a man who was spying out for them started shouting: 'There he is, there he is!'—he was hiding in a bush. So they hunted about, and they went right past him a dozen times and never saw him. But in the end they found him because their informer called out: 'There! He's in there!' So they hauled him out—they dragged him out by his foot, like a ewe or a lamb. One of them said: 'Is he alive or dead?' 'Dead,' says another, and so my father ups and says: 'Not half so dead as you, you rotten bunch of bastards!' and he spat at them.

He got three years, one month, and fifteen days—he counted up the days himself. Then they let him out, but only under supervision—he had to stay at home all day, so he couldn't go out and earn his living. Three years under police supervision. I went out to work, though, but I was still very young and not much good at the work, so we always went hungry. I looked after five cows for a man and got half the milk money from one cow and a share in the other four.

I used to have a bath in the summer when I went down to the sea to wash the animals, the sheep and cows. In winter I didn't wash at all. I didn't go right into the sea, though—I stayed standing on the beach, because I couldn't swim. Once, I took the cows into a field which belonged to the man who gave away my father to the police that time, and he ran after me and tried to beat me, but I got away. Another time I met him, he pulled out a knife and would have cut my throat, but again I managed to escape. As I was running away, my uncles came up and asked me where I'd left the animals. It turned out that this man was driving the animals off to the village himself, so my uncles went and got them back. Another time, they had a fight with him.

I never went to school—never once, not even for a single day. None of my family have ever been to school. I don't know of anyone in my family who can read or write.

Last night I dreamt about my uncles. They were dressing a white skin, a sheepskin. And then I had that dream about the cows chewing the grass.

What are the stars? How do you expect *me* to know! There's the moon which shines instead of the sun at night. But I think I do understand the stars, really. At night when they come out, I can see millions and millions of them up there. They must be made of some kind of smoke—all the smoke in the world, which rises up into the sky, and sometimes at night you can see it and other times you can't. The moon's made of sky, and the sky is made of the smoke which rises up from the earth. And sometimes in the morning the moon's still there when the sun gets up. The stars move across the sky all night long—they never stay still. Then when day comes they always go in. It's just like the animals going into their shed at the end of the day when it's time to rest. We all do the same—stars, animals, and human beings.

I've had a dream about fire, too—what does that mean? And about a river of filthy water, rushing along very fast: what does it mean when you dream about that? I was terrified of the fire, and I was running away—but only in my dream. Of course when I'm awake I'm not frightened of fire. And I've also dreamt that people were trying to drown me. They pushed me under the water, and I tried to shout out, but they beat me down with sticks.

The earth is an island, and all round it there's sea. I know, because when I first went to prison I was taken out in a boat to the Colombaia, from Tràpani, and that convinced me that the earth is earth, and that we're in the middle of an island. I said to myself then: 'If there's sea all round here, too, as well as over by Castellammare, then that means the earth must be an island.' I could see that the Colombaia was an island, that time they took me out there in handcuffs, and so I realised just what an island was.

What is Italy? Well, this is Italy, Italy's here too. I think this is all Italy, even the Ucciardone prison here. This is the prison, but it's Italy as well. And Italy's in Sicily too. The difference between Sicily and Italy? Well, when they say 'Giornale di Sicilia' they mean the newspaper of all the Parties.

Since I came to prison, I've had things I never had before: a bed, for instance, with sheets and blankets and a mattress and pillows—d'you suppose I'd ever had those before? I know I was born in the village because they told me so, my father told me so himself. But otherwise I've always stayed out in the country. I used to stand and look at the houses from outside, from a distance, but as for going inside—what business of mine was it to go inside? Was I the owner? When the police came to arrest me, I was out with the cows. I saw them coming and I tried to escape, but they caught me there among the cows.

I do know how to shoot. If I shoot at a man, I get him. How I learnt was from this bloke. I saw his gun, and I said: 'Will you give me that stick?' and he says: 'Stick? This is a gun.' So I said to him: 'Show me how to work it, then,' because I'd seen him fire and hit. So he handed it to me, and I aimed at two prickly-pears, and hit them. How he taught me was by holding the gun for me while I pulled the trigger.

I can catch rabbits with my bare hands, in summer, when

they hide among the stones. I used to catch them and break their necks, then gut them and flay them and roast them over the fire—just like that, without any salt or oil. Who would I have got oil from? I'd take a couple of stones and knock them together and light my fire with the sparks. Firestones, those are called. Then I'd put the rabbit over the fire, and as soon as I saw it was getting brown on one side, I'd turn it over and brown the other side, and then when it was done I'd eat it. Sometimes I've even eaten rabbits raw. I used to eat raw slugs, too, and snails from their shells, and wild asparagus. And little wild olives. And wild radishes. And borage, whenever I could find it—I like borage. I used to eat that roots and all. And wherever there was water I used to catch frogs, and skin them and roast them. I caught foxes, too, big ones and little ones: I used to make snares and hide them at the entrance to foxes' earths. Once I caught a great big vixen—as big as that, it was—and it bit me in the shoulder: but I picked up a stone and smashed its skull.

Wild dogs, too, I used to eat, whenever I could catch them. I killed them by flinging them down the side of the mountain again and again till they were dead. Sometimes the crows would fly down, wanting to eat the dog themselves, but I threw stones to drive them off. I used to take the eggs of goldfinches and robins to suck. And I ate hedgehogs, too. I used to lay straw outside their holes, and when they got in among the straw I would kill them with a stick. They're very good to eat, hedgehogs. And of course rabbits are good too. I used to skin the hedgehog—not very well, but as well as I could with my bare hands—and then cook it on the fire at night for my supper. I didn't have any bread, you see. I used to eat a whole hedgehog in one go.

When I was in prison on the Colombaia, they gave me a bit of schooling. They showed me an egg and told me that was 'o'. Then an 'o' with a little leg on it, and that was 'a'. Then they showed me 'i'—and that was all.

What would I do if I could choose? Well, I'd like to go on looking after animals. I'd like to be able to count, and to reckon up money. And also I'd like to be able to work and earn money by buying things and then selling them at a profit. For instance, I could buy a pair of shoes for a hundred lire and sell them for two hundred. How much does a pair of shoes cost? In my whole life, I've only had four pairs of shoes. When my father came out of prison he got me my first pair, and then when they split he gave me another pair. These rubber ones I'm wearing now were given me by one of my cousins when I had to go to court. I had another pair before this, but they had hobnails and so I kept slipping and falling over on the cement floor and on the steps. Every time I fell over the warders glared at me, so after a bit I sent them home and went barefoot again.

I'll tell you what we ought to do to make the world a better place. If we could do away with all the police barracks, we'd be a lot better off. But then, someone'll say, we'd all start killing each other: well, maybe we would—but at least we'd be reasonable and only kill people who deserved to be killed.

Yes, of course there's someone at the head of Italy. Who? Mussolini, I think. Then there's all the lawyers over us—all these lawyers and magistrates on our backs gobbling up all our money. I'll tell you what we ought to do to all these people who exploit us: kill them, and then set fire to them and burn them all up so that no one would even be able to find their ashes.

The difference between my life up in the mountains and life here in town? Well, I've grown wild out in the country, and if I come down into the town no one wants to have anything to do with me. I'm different from them, you see. A town man can read and write, and can work and earn his living, and he knows how to behave, how to get along with other people. Living in town, a man's always in company: whereas up in the mountains you never see a soul. It's good being with other people—but only if you can talk properly: if you can't, if you don't know how to behave rightly, they'll kick you out, they'll kill you. If a bloke doesn't know how to get on with them, they'll pick a quarrel with him and get him arrested and put in prison, or under police supervision. No one'll have anything to do with a penniless fellow like me—they're only interested in trotting after the rich ones, the ones with power. It's them that ought to get killed, not us poor blokes.

If I could have a wish, I'd like to learn to read and write—but I'd still want to go on looking after animals. They may not be able to talk, but they've got their own language, and they can understand. Instead of speaking, they say: 'Uuuu—uuuuh . . .' If they're getting into mischief, I only have to give them a shout and they stop what they're doing at once. If they don't take any notice the first time, you have to take a stick to them, or hit them on the horns with a pebble, and that gives them a fright and teaches them not to do it again.

Animals can't tell you things themselves, so you have to watch and notice things like when they get thirsty. In May, now, and right through the summer, they're always thirsty, because the grass gets all dried up. They can't tell you they're thirsty, but if you're looking after them you have to pay attention to that sort of thing, otherwise they'll soon begin to grow weak and thin. I get on much better with the cows and the sheep and goats than I do with human beings. If I look after a cow properly, she pays me back by giving me milk: I respect her, and she respects me. But with human beings, quite the opposite —it's them that milk me! I know how to deal with animals, you see—with cows, and sheep, and goats: but I just don't know how to get along with people. Animals have always been nicer to me than people have. I've had some animals so tame they'd stay with me all the time. Once, I had a kid and a lamb that used to follow me around wherever I went. I used to share my bread with them sometimes—if I had any myself, that is. They even ate *pasta* and sauce with me once or twice, they got so tame. I was very fond of them; and because I was kind to them they stayed near me and followed me around wherever I went. If I went inside the byre, they followed me in, and if I went down to the sea, then they came with me there, too. If I called them, they would answer in their own language, and then come running up and start skipping round me.

I like to have company, but I can't bear the sort of company where both sides hate each other. But of course sometimes you'll even get an animal that hates you—there was one bull that hated me. And there've been one or two cows that hated me, as well: I had one that used to kick, and there was another one that used to go and muck up the fig trees and never took any notice when I called her. And then there was one very greedy one who was always running off to look for food—later she produced a great fat calf.

But all the same, even if some beasts can hate you too, they're still better than human beings. At least you can tame animals —or if you get one you really can't tame, you can sell it. Or you can even kill it, without having to pay any penalty! If an animal is treacherous or untrustworthy, you can just get rid of it. With human beings, though, it's much more risky getting rid of them, because if you're found out—I mean, say I killed you or you killed me, we'd have to pay for it! And besides, cows can't band together and plot to do me down, whereas human beings can—they can plot together to harm me, and take the food out of my mouth, and even take away my freedom.

I've never had any friends as close as that kid and that lamb. I never saw much of my father—he was always away, either in the army, or in prison, or confined to the village under supervision. I do know him a bit, though, my father. And my mother and brothers are fond of me too. But no one has ever loved me like that kid and that lamb did—not even God himself. I watched them being born, the kid and the lamb, and I used to feed them out of my own hand. I got to love them so much—I still think about them all the time, the way they used to follow me about. When they were tiny, I held them up under the cow to suck, and they used to follow me around just like puppies.

I don't know why, but I got to love that kid and that lamb terribly. The kid used to dance and play round me. My brothers had each other to play with, but I never had anyone but the kid.

And then I had to sell the kid to buy food. For a month I couldn't bring myself to do it—I needed the money badly, but I wanted to keep the kid. 'Shall I sell it—or shall I keep it?' I kept asking myself. I wanted both. It was a white kid, but its head and neck were dappled with red. Its eyes were just like a person's—just like yours; and it had a little tufted tail. As it grew bigger, its horns began to curve backwards. I'd got so fond of it—I really loved it—I couldn't bear the thought of parting with it. But in the end I had to. I sold it, and bought a kilo of bread and a kilo of fish. But all the time I was eating, I kept thinking about the kid. For two days after that I couldn't eat at all for thinking about it, and I couldn't stop crying. Then I went back to work, but for eight months after that I never stopped thinking about the kid—and even now I still keep thinking about it.

My mother was fond of me, too. Whenever I left home to go up into the mountains, she would say: 'Be careful now, and mind you don't slip and fall. Do your work well and honestly. Keep yourself to yourself, and don't have anything to do with men who might hurt you.' When I was going a long way away, or when I was going away for a long time—six months, say—she used to kiss me goodbye. If she had any bread, she would always give me some, but of course when she had none herself she couldn't!

I've had two Christmases and two Easters in prison. Before, I would sometimes spend them up in the mountains, and sometimes at home.

I'd never seen a film till I came to prison. The first time I saw one, I couldn't make out what it was all about—men waving swords, horses galloping about all over the place. I saw a circus once—there was a lady who balanced on a big ball, and a horse that walked along a narrow plank. The first time I went in a train was when I was eleven. We were going to see my father who was in jail on the Colombaia, but when we got there the sea was so rough we couldn't cross, so we just had to wait at the platform and go home again. The second time was when I broke my arm falling off the horse. And the third time was coming here to prison.

Political Parties? There are three or four: the Socialists; the Democrats—that's the priests' party; the Monarchists; the Communists ... They ought to cut the heads off everyone in the priests' party and play *pallone* with them. The Monarchists are the rich ones, the landowners, who keep their heels on the necks of us poor people and bleed us white. I've no use for any party, I don't belong to any of them—I can't vote, because I've been to prison. I'd like to see the whole lot of them lined up against the wall and shot. These lawyers and all these damned magistrates never speak a word of truth—I know, because I've listened to people's talk and picked up a thing or two.

What sort of government have they got in America and Russia? The same as ours. What's Russia? A little island. China? Never heard of it. D'you mean a bunch of grapes?'[1]

It's all on account of two bunches of grass that I'm here in prison. I'd gone into this field to pick some grass, and there was this boy watching, and he gave a whistle and at once a man came running up, and I saw a stone flying through the air at me. I took to my heels at once, and ran off, with the cow galloping along in front of me. Then the police came for me. The first time they came, I was mucking out the byre when I heard the sound of the horses' hooves. They wanted to take me off to the barracks, and they tried to handcuff me, but I wasn't going!

Then they came again. The second time, I was milking the cows, and they caught me and made me walk between their horses. They took me down to the police barracks, and when we got there they threatened me with their knives, and beat me about the shoulders with a stick, and kicked me. They wrote things down—not with a pen, though: it was some damned thing that went tin-tin-tin—I don't know what it was. Then they made me put a cross on the paper, and then they let me go.

Four months later, though, they came and arrested me and put me in prison. They sent me out to the Colombaia. Then I was put on trial, and sentenced to four years and twenty days. They'd asked the judge for six years. They asked me if I wanted to appeal, but I was crying so hard I couldn't see a thing. And now here I am in the Ucciardone, waiting for my appeal to be heard, but they keep having to put it off because the injured party—the man whose grass I picked—never turns up.

[1] 'La Cina' sounds like 'racina'.

# Santo, an agricultural trade-unionist

THESE *pagliari*[1] here were put up when we were children by the *mezzadri*[2]—but even though they'd built them themselves, the landowner still made them each pay a levy of a dozen hens a year for the right to live in them. And every time he came to stay at Túdia, he made the *mezzadri* send their womenfolk along to the big house to work as unpaid servants.

In the early days, there used to be about two hundred *mezzadri* on this estate. Sometimes, they would be going out at about four o'clock in the morning—to the threshing floor, say, or to collect the seed-corn—when all of a sudden they'd see the doors opening onto the balcony of the master's house, and they'd have to bolt out of the way: you see, the master had a nice little habit of peeing over the edge of the balcony, never mind who was down below! Of course if a peasant had done a thing like that, there would have been a public scandal.

Don Eugenio used to keep peacocks along with his poultry. The Duke of S. kept some in his courtyard, too, to give his place more of an air of pomp and elegance.

When the time came round to divide up the produce, the *mezzadro* had to go along to the estate offices (he still has to do this today, of course), to report on the crops and give an account of everything he'd spent throughout the year on seed and so on. Often the owner would deliberately make mistakes in his reckoning—but as soon as the tenant opened his mouth to protest, the owner would dismiss him by getting up from his seat saying: 'That will be all, then—good day to you.'

Now D.'s heirs have raised the money to buy the estate, by

[1] *Pagliari*: primitive huts made of mud and bamboo.
[2] *Mezzadri*: peasant farmers who instead of rent pay the landowner a share of their crops.

forcing the tenants to pay more than they lawfully should: five *pagliari* were burnt down once, and every now and again another one gets burnt, as a warning.

I came to Túdia in 1941: I was a tenant farmer, but I had six head of oxen of my own. When the landowner, Cesare D., suggested we should have the beasts valued and then go shares in them, I agreed. A few months later, he brought me the contract—but he'd had the beasts valued at the price that suited him, far less than they were worth, so at first I refused to sign. But then he began to threaten me by saying that if I didn't like his terms I would have to take the animals off his land, and as I had nowhere else to go if I was evicted, I was forced to accept.

The following spring when the time came round for dividing up the forage, he wanted to take a higher proportion than I'd ever agreed to, more than his legal due; but this time I stood firm, and from then on he had it in for me. One fine day, the notice to quit arrived. I was out at the time, but when I got home I found my wife in a fearful state. 'Look what the land-lord's sent!' she cried. I didn't know where to turn to for advice —at that time I didn't know about trades unions. But I asked various people what I should do, and was told to go to the Communist Party headquarters down in Petralia Sottana and they would help me defend my rights. So I saddled my mare one day and rode all the way down to Petralia—it took six and a half hours. When I got there, I asked for the Party headquarters, and was sent to see this student, who was the son of the miller. As soon as he'd heard my story, he sent me on to Dr. B. How-ever, when I got to the Doctor's house, he wasn't there—he was out on his rounds, so I had to wait about two hours. When he came back and found me waiting there, seeing I was a stranger, before I'd had time to say anything he asked me in a very polite and friendly way what he could do for me. I told him about the notice to quit, and he said: 'You just stay put: don't you budge out of your house, even if he sends along a squad of *carabinieri* to evict you. Meanwhile I'll write to Palermo, and as soon as I hear I'll let you know exactly what you must do.'

Then he took down my address, and we shook hands, and I set off back to Túdia.

On the 28th of June when I was up in Petralia Soprana for the Feast of Saint Peter, I noticed some posters stuck up on the walls, so I read them. (I got as far as the fifth elementary class at school.) They were all about the new laws on the distribution of produce—signed by Gullo, Minister of Agriculture. I got hold of a few of these posters, and when I went back to Túdia I stuck them up around the place, and explained to the other *mezzadri* about this new law (which anyone could read for himself from the posters) fixing the owner's share of our produce at 40 per cent.

Well, a short while before the reaping was finished, the owner arrives at Túdia and orders us to start threshing at once. This was the first time he'd ever taken it into his head to come and chivvy us over the threshing. Only a few of them were ready to begin, in fact, but as soon as their corn was cleaned he demanded his usual share, taking no notice at all of the new laws.

When the *mezzadri* refused to give him more than his legal due, he threatened to send for the *carabinieri* and have them all arrested. So they came to me, along with two other *mezzadri* from the L . . . fief, and this really gave me heart. To make quite certain from the Party that we were acting rightly, I rode down with these other *mezzadri* to Petralia—thirteen hours on horseback, that meant: six and a half hours each way.

Comrade N. Giovanni and Comrade L. came back with us from Petralia. We set off late, so we had to spend the night at Le Fontanelle, up on top of the mountain, in a cowshed; and it made a real impression on me to see that young student lying down there in the cowshed along with us—and not even lying on the straw, but on the bare earth. What reason had he to throw in his lot with us? I couldn't get over the fact that he was willing to share our hardships. It made such an impression on me—I won't ever forget him.

Next morning, the *mezzadro* who lived up there brought us some milk to drink, and then we set off again for Túdia, and made our way to the estate offices. By this time a crowd of about three hundred peasants and *mezzadri* had gathered outside, and by the time I got there (I was the last to arrive) I was told that the Comrades had already gone up into the big house to see the owner.

'Nothing will come of it, though,' they were grumbling. 'It'll be the same old story—they'll sell out to him as usual.' So I tried to reassure them. 'We ought to trust them,' I said: 'they're decent, honest men who've come here to defend the rights of us workers. They're on our side, and they're not going to be bribed by anybody.'

I'd just started trying to make my way through the crowd, when I heard someone call my name. It was my brother. We hadn't spoken to each other for two years, on account of some family quarrel. 'What on earth d'you think you're doing?' he said—you see, he knew there was a detachment of *carabinieri* in Túdia, and he was afraid I'd be arrested. That made me stop and think for a moment—but then I said to myself: 'Why shouldn't I go? I haven't done anything wrong, so why should I be arrested?' And on I went into the big house.

When the landlord saw me coming up the stairs he came down to meet me, and shook my hand in a friendly way, and slapped me on the back, and said confidentially: 'Come on now, Santo, let's behave like the sensible fellows we are, eh?' Then he showed me into the big room, and there I saw our leaders, along with a number of *carabinieri* and their sergeant.

As soon as I came in, the Comrades said: 'Listen—Don Cèsare has agreed to split the produce fifty-fifty with the *mezzadri* for the time being, since the talks between Aldisio and Gullo are still going on, and then when the talks are over he'll refund whatever may be due to you. Otherwise, he says, we'll have to await the outcome of the talks before we get any at all.'

So I replied: 'Comrades, since this noble gentleman has millions in the bank, of course it doesn't really matter to him whether we split the produce now or later: but we *must* have our share now. It may seem a small amount to bother about, but for us poor folk with families to support it's a matter of life and death.'

Then the landlord turns to me and says: 'Don't you trust me then?' 'No!' I told him: how could I trust him, I said, when he'd cheated me so often over the distribution of the crops. Over and over again, he'd taken more than his fair share; and then, though he'd promised to give me back what was due to me, I would have to go up time and time again to the estate offices to ask for it back, and always he would have some excuse—he'd lost the key to the storehouse, or he was too busy to attend to me. 'Goodness knows how often I've had to walk those four miles there and back,' I wound up, 'and each time I felt as humiliated as if I'd been begging for charity.'

Then he said: 'You've received your notice to quit, haven't you?'

'Yes,' I replied, 'and since you've mentioned it, I'd be glad if you would explain now, in front of these gentlemen here, the reason why you're turning me out.'

'You're a good fellow,' he says, 'but we just don't seem to be able to hit it off together, you and I.'

'I'm sorry you're not satisfied with me,' I answered him, 'but it makes no difference: I, Santo S., intend to stay here at Túdia as long as the law permits. After all, it's not as if we have to sleep in the same bed!'

With that, I went out again and joined the others. Then Don Cèsare came out onto the balcony and addressed the crowd of peasants waiting below. He said he would split the corn fifty-fifty with us *mezzadri*, but promised to refund whatever might be due to us when the talks between Aldisio and Gullo were concluded. Then I asked if I might say a word. 'We suggest, sir, that you take 40 per cent and leave us 60 per cent,' I said. 'And in any case, this provisional distribution only affects a fraction of the crop, since the bulk of it isn't even threshed yet.' He still refused, though. So then I said: 'Very well, there'll be no distribution today, and we will not thresh the rest until a contract has been signed that will guarantee our getting our lawful percentage.'

I'm ashamed to tell you what happened in the end. We gave in. But what else could we do, when he started threatening us all with eviction?

In 1947, during the general strike, the peasants were so fed up with the law which obliged them to hand over so much corn yearly to the State (which often left them with none at all for themselves) that they took advantage of the situation and broke into the Town Hall and ransacked the offices of the Agricultural Board and burnt all their papers. I was trying to calm them down and prevent any further incidents, but the *Carabinieri* came and arrested me, along with twenty others, and hauled us off to prison. Eighteen months in prison! And for my family, eighteen months without me, cut off out there in the country-side. Then after we'd been tried and had appealed, we were sentenced to four months. And all the time I was in prison, Don Cèsare did everything he could to terrorise my family into clearing out. In the end he promised my wife a hundred thousand lire if she'd agree to quit of her own accord. But my wife refused to budge.

The year after that, it was the hay. This time, though, it was the new owner, Don Vittorio. Exactly the same thing happened when it came to the distribution of the hay. He made it clear he was not going to stick to the laws, and the struggle began all over again. Then when we'd finished threshing the beans, I and one or two other *mezzadri* offered to give him his lawful percentage—but again he wouldn't agree.

On the 13th of July, at four o'clock in the afternoon, we leaders went to the Prefecture; however, since the gentlemen refused to appear, we were unable to lodge our complaint. The peasants were waiting anxiously to hear what had happened, but just as we got back, along came Don Vittorio and the sergeant of the *carabinieri* in a Fiat 1400. The car drew up, and Don Vittorio called me over, and whispered confidentially: 'You take your share, Santo, but don't bother about the others—let them look after their own affairs.'

'They must get theirs first,' I said: 'I'm not taking my share till they've all got theirs.'

He drew himself up and gave me some pompous answer or other, so I retorted: 'You only get away with lording it over us like this because you're backed up by certain members of the police who—instead of enforcing the law—are simply protecting your interests.' Then he and the sergeant drove on, and I went and joined the other *mezzadri*.

A few minutes later, back came the Fiat, driven by Don Vittorio's chauffeur: he told me to get in and come along with him, as the sergeant wanted a word with me. I replied: 'I'm not obliged to go, but since my conscience is quite clear, I've no objection.'

As soon as I got there, the sergeant asked me: 'Signor Santo, whatever made you say what you said just now?' and I replied: 'Because it's true, and you yourself are the living proof of it.'

Then Don Vittorio asked us to come into his office, and the same old argument started about the percentages. Presently the cook appeared at the door and announced that dinner was ready. I got up to go, but Don Vittorio said: 'Please, you must do me the honour of being my guest this evening.' So I stayed; and all through the meal he kept handing me things like a waiter, and saying: 'Come on, Santo, help yourself! Have another drink, Santo! We're still good friends, eh?'—patting me on the back—'We're the best of good fellows, aren't we, Santo?' and pressing me to eat and drink. It was as much as I could do not to laugh—I'd never been treated like this in all my life: on the contrary, whenever Don Vittorio got the *mezzadri* to shift beans or chick-peas from one storehouse to another for him, he never condescended to offer us so much as a glass of water!

'Eat up, Santo. Come on, have another drink, Santo. Listen, I like you. You seem to me to be a decent sort of chap'—winking at me—'Now, you do the sensible thing, and don't let your family down. I don't mind if you keep all your crop, the whole lot. And if you still haven't enough, I can even let you have some more.' But I was on my guard: I'd been careful to avoid drinking the wine, as I didn't want to fall for his trick.

In the meantime, the factor had already typed out the agree-

D

ment, and as soon as the meal was over, we went back into the office. Don Vittorio sat down, signed the agreement, then passed it to me. But I refused to sign it. Then the *carabinieri* sergeant, who was still with us, ordered me at least to read it. I obeyed, but as soon as I had read it, I flung it down on the table in front of Don Vittorio.

The sergeant drew himself up, and said in his best official manner: 'Am I to take it, then, that you refuse to sign?' 'I refuse,' I said, 'and you can't force me.'

'Then I authorise the landowner to take four witnesses and to go and sieze the whole crop and put it in his own storehouse.'

I went to the door.

'Wait a minute!' the owner called after me: 'Wouldn't you like a lift in the car?'

'No thank you,' I called back: 'I'd rather go on my own two feet.' And I went out and joined the other peasants who'd gathered outside the house.

About eight o'clock that same evening, the Superintendent himself drove up to my house with a vanload of police. There was quite a party of us inside—one man was playing the accordion, and the rest of us were singing. The police surrounded the house; and while some of them came in and arrested us, me and thirteen other men, the rest of them went and confiscated our beans. We were driven to the Resuttana barracks, where we spent the night, and in the morning we were taken to the Polizia Generosa prison. We were interrogated that same evening, and two days later we were transferred to the prison at Tèrmini Imerese. After eight days, we were provisionally released; and when finally we appeared in court, we were all acquitted.

A week later, exactly the same thing happened over the distribution of the corn: this time I was twenty-eight days in prison before my trial—and again I was acquitted, since I hadn't committed any offence. But of course Don Vittorio took advantage of my absence to adjust the distribution in his favour and had fourteen quintals of my corn carried into his granary.

Then at last a year came when the produce was divided up

according to the law: 60 per cent for us, 40 per cent for him. Only once, though—that was the only time I've won. Because, you see, fighting him single-handed like this, I'm just too weak— I can't do it alone, I'm powerless. Sometimes I used to organise meetings—but I'd always be in such a fever of anxiety. 'Be on your guard!' I'd say: 'For goodness sake be careful, or they'll arrest us all—and me first!' Then they'd swear that as long as there was one man left at large, the struggle would still go on. But time and time again, the sight of the police or the *carabinieri* threw them into such a panic that they'd go back to the owner and say: 'It's Santo who's to blame—it's all his fault, he needs his head cut off! It's him who goads us into doing all this!' And they'd even take him up a basket of eggs as a peace offering.

It's not that they don't realise and appreciate what's being done to help them. But if you talk to one of them alone, he'll say: 'The trouble is, there's no unity.'

'But if you believe in what we're doing,' I tell him, 'why not stand by me, and that'll make two of us. Unity doesn't grow on trees, you know!'

'All right, you can count on me!' they say. But then when I turn round, I find there's no one behind me, or hardly anyone.

The police keep accusing us of being agitators. And sooner or later . . . Listen: only five miles from here, Epifanio Li Puma was killed—murdered by the Mafia of the fief. Still, in the end some of that land was expropriated and distributed among the peasants.

# Rosario: rural industry

FIVE or six different kinds of greenstuff that are good to eat grow wild in the countryside. I mean stuff that no one sows—things that seed themselves.

When you go out gathering, you just walk along and pick whatever you come across. You have to get up early in the morning, about three or four or five o'clock, say, depending on the time of year, and how far you have to go. You go out into the countryside, and sometimes you have to walk six or seven miles before you find anything. There's nothing to be found along the roadsides: either it's all covered with dust—and of course it's no use if it's all dusty—or else people who've passed that way have already picked everything worth having and taken it home to make soup. Or else it's all been eaten or trampled on and spoilt by the cows.

When you get to where the stuff grows, you may have to walk two or three miles or more before you fill a sack, which will give you about two hundred little bunches. Usually I go picking with another man, or even two or three others. We can give each other a hand, then, and anyway it's best not to go alone in case you land in any sort of trouble. Quite likely the owner of a piece of land will tick you off for walking over his crops, or else he won't let you pick anything because he says he needs it all himself.

When a couple of us go out collecting together, we usually agree to pool everything we pick and share the takings. That way it works out all right. But if you're out with someone and you haven't made this sort of agreement, then you're anxious all the time, and you keep looking round at him, and waste all your time wondering whether he's going to get his sack filled first, and whether his patch of greenstuff is better than the one you're on. Then if you see, say, a clump of wild cabbages, you have to rush to get it before he does. Sometimes, though, you can't find enough to fill your sack.

It's the same sort of rush when you're gathering snails. If you want to collect five or six pounds of them in the early morning before the sun is up, you really have to be smart and use your eyes all the time. Before you pick up the first one, you'll already have your eye on the next; then you go for that one, but while you're picking it up you've already spotted another over there: you go darting about all over the place—you can't afford to waste time.

You have to make sure the greenstuff you pick is in good condition, and not full of worms. Some of the worms are so tiny you can hardly see them, so you have to look very carefully. At this time of year, for instance, all the fennel is crawling with worms—well, not every bit, of course, but almost. There are two sorts of wild fennel, mountain fennel and donkey fennel: the donkey sort isn't edible, it smells too rank. They're very much alike, but we can tell them apart because the leaves are slightly different.

When we're out collecting, we bundle all the different sorts of greenstuff into the sack together. (I'm still talking about the kinds that grow wild, of course: chicory, wild cabbages, fennel, wild asparagus, borage and so on.) Then when our sacks are stuffed full, we go back to the village. As soon as I get home, my wife fetches water. You need a lot of water—you must clean it really thoroughly, otherwise no one'll buy it. Then I sort it all out, putting each different kind in its own pile, and then I tie it into bunches. If I decide to sell them to the wholesaler, I get three or four lire the bunch: if I decide to sell them myself next day, I can get fifteen lire for a couple of bunches, or five lire for one—but that means I lose a day's gathering, so it's hardly worth it.

When you go out after snails, you have to get up very early in the morning—two or three o'clock at the latest. Because, you see, you've got to be out there on the spot before it begins to get light. As soon as the sun comes up, the snails disappear—they go underground and don't come out again all day. If it's a dull cloudy morning, you can still find some creeping around up till about eleven o'clock. After that, though, you won't find any at all—they don't come out again for the rest of the day. There aren't any snails in the vineyards—I suppose that's because they're hoed four or five times a year. You find them on fallow land, or in fields sown with beans, or corn, or sulla, and so on. And you find lots near water. You get large numbers of them when there's been a heavy dew, too. But all these new chemical fertilisers they're using on the fields are killing off the snails—all these ammonia salts and stuff they're sprinkling all over the place. It's killing them. You can walk for miles these days and not find any.

These last few days, I've been eel-fishing over at Corleone. About half way between Contessa and Corleone we have to start getting the baskets ready. We use ten or twelve worms to each basket, threaded on a wire. When the baits are all set, we take the baskets down to the river and made them fast to something on the bank, and throw them in where the water is deepest. During the day we don't catch any eels: they only come out to feed at night. But next morning (we sleep on the spot, of course, there on the river bank)—next morning, as soon as we wake up, we go and pull in our baskets to see what luck we've had. If we haven't caught any eels, we have to go on and try a different stretch of the river. If we're in luck, though, we may find four or five eels in one basket, or even six or seven. But it's just as likely we'll find none at all. And in any case, you only ever catch the little eels: you'll never find one over about six or seven ounces in the basket. These days, though, there are hardly any eels left at all, big or small: they've started throwing poison into the river to catch them, and that kills off even the eggs.

When the water is very low (and as long as we're on a stretch that hasn't been poisoned, of course), we can catch eels with forks, ordinary table forks, tied to the end of a stick. We turn over the stones and try to stab them before they dart away. But they move like lightning! Often they're too quick for us, and then we have to follow them a few yards downstream—

they always try to escape downstream—and start turning over the stones again. We always go eel-fishing in twos or threes. And we can only do it in summer, when the river's fairly shallow: in winter it gets far too deep.

Another thing we hunt for is *babbalucedde*—they're a kind of tiny little snail which you find on twigs and stalks. You see them often on thistles, all stuck together in clusters, one on top of the other. We start collecting them in June, and go on through July and August, until the rainy season begins. Then the big snails start again, so of course there's no need to bother with these tiny ones any more. These little *babbalucedde* live on the thistles, and they always seem to stay up among the spikes, and never dry up like other snails. You cook them in the ordinary way, just like the big ones, and then suck them out of their shells.

That's how we live. We go wherever the wind blows us, and as we walk we gather whatever we find.

When we're getting frogs ready for market, we cut off their heads and feet with shears, and skin them, and gut them. Then we break the legs to make them swell out. They look so tempting, all cleaned and prepared like that, with their nice plump thighs, that as soon as people see them they say: 'I'll have a kilo of those, please!' Even when we've cut off their heads and feet and skinned them and cleaned them out and broken their legs, the frogs still go on moving. We soak them in water for a couple of hours, and then they're ready to be sold. They fetch two hundred lire a kilo, cleaned and prepared like that. We catch them in the daytime, but we have to wait till night to skin them—you mustn't kill them too soon: if you leave a skinned frog more than about six hours, it'll begin to stink.

When I see the sort of lives animals lead, I often think to myself that really they're no different from us. We all eat each other up—I may eat one of them, but they eat other creatures too. Animals' lives are just as much of a struggle as ours.

Sometimes in the evening, I look up at the stars—and specially when I'm sleeping out at night, like when we go eel-fishing—I look up at the stars, and I think to myself: 'Is the world real?' and I wonder if perhaps it's not real at all. When things are going reasonably well, then I do believe in Jesus, and there are even times when I'd be willing to kill anyone who spoke ill of him. But there are times, too, when I just can't believe in God at all. 'If there really is a God,' I say to myself, 'then why doesn't he send me work?'

If only I had a proper job . . . Sometimes I get so desperate I feel like hanging myself—but then I think of my children: what would they do without me? All the same, though . . . You know, I'm afraid I'll go out of my mind soon, if I can't find any proper work.

I feel wretched when I'm skinning these frogs—I hate having to kill them, but I can't help it: I have to kill them in order to live. But I feel so sorry for them, I hate doing it. As soon as I get hold of a frog, it knows it's going to die. I'm certain of that. What makes me so certain? Well, when you take it in your hand ready to cut off its head and feet, the frog empties its bladder—just like a man does when he's terribly afraid. So I'm certain it knows it's going to die. Any animal does: whatever animal you catch, as soon as it feels your hands round it, it begins to tremble all over. Sometimes when I take a young bird out of the nest I can feel its heart beating like a little bell. It knows its last hour has come: it's just the same as if you pointed a revolver at a man. Even snails: don't think that just because the snail is one of the lowest sorts of creature it can't realise what's happening to it. I'm certain even a snail knows, in its own way. I'm quite sure every animal knows when it's going to die.

When you catch an eel, before you cut off its head to pull the guts out, it opens its mouth and gasps for breath and tries to bite you with its tiny little teeth. It flaps and thrashes about till it's got no breath left—it can't breathe out of water. Then you cut its head off, from the under side upwards, and then you make a cross-cut to pull the guts through.

When we're skinning frogs, there are four of us round the basket: my wife skins them, one of my cousins cuts off the heads with the shears, my other cousin snips off their feet, and I gut them and break their legs. And sometimes, to pass the time, we pretend we're in court and have a kind of trial. The cousin who cuts off their heads gets thirty years, because he's the murderer; my wife gets twenty years for being accessory after the fact; the cousin who cuts off their feet—she gets twenty years too; and as for me, I get life imprisonment because it's all my fault that the frogs are being killed in the first place.

When you've chopped off a frog's head, its eyes seem to go on watching you from the table, as if they were still alive—it's just like the way the eyes in a portrait seem to follow you about. With all those cut-off heads lying around, it's like a massacre. If you were to see all those heads lined up in rows . . . When I first started doing it, I can't tell you how terrible it made me feel. But now . . . Last year I killed a hundred and fifty kilos of frogs. I'm so hardened to it now that if one jumps out of my hand and escapes when I'm in a hurry to get the cleaning done, I get in quite a rage with it, and hit it on the head with a stick till it's dead, or else I kill it by dashing it on the ground.

Those rich devils who let us starve to death in order to keep all their land and property and money for themselves, and never spare us so much as a thought—I wish they could have some of the nightmares I have: basketfuls of cut-off heads. Only for them it wouldn't be frogs' heads: it would be the heads of all the men and women whose deaths they are responsible for. I wish they could dream of all those eyes watching them . . .

Well, now I've told you what I do to scrape up some sort of a living for my family. I've tried my hand at everything. I was eight when I left school—I got as far as the second elementary class—and ever since then I've managed as best I could by doing whatever came my way. Thank God, so far I've never been in trouble with the police. My family's daily bread is honestly earned, by the sweat of my brow. I work far harder than any labourer or factory hand: and, what's more, I have to use my brains all the time, too. You have to plan everything: one day you go to one place, the next day you may have to go somewhere quite different. I always work out my plans in the evening.

I enjoy this sort of work, I always have. But it's so exhausting —and why should I be wearing myself out like this? What I'd really like is a regular, steady job. I'd like to be able to get up in the morning and know exactly where I'm going to be working all day. It's not that I'm not willing to work hard—but I know I could do something better than this. I've got a brain, I know I could learn to do something better. Of course it would take time: I'd seem just like a block of wood at first, but after a fortnight or so I'd begin to pick things up all right. Five years ago, when I came back after my military service, I started doing labouring jobs: but the first year I only managed to get three months' work; then I had four months' work in the second, and six months' in the third; only three months again in the fourth year, and five months last year. The rest of the time I went out gathering greenstuff in the countryside: *verdurari,* we're called.

Another thing I pick sometimes is capers. They're the flower buds of a plant which you find in rocky valleys—the bushes grow out of the rocks, not out of the earth. If you leave these buds to open, though, you'll get a kind of little cucumber later on which you can split and sprinkle with salt and lay out to dry in the sun.

When I was seventeen, I used to go out looking for scraps of coal and charcoal. I only did that for a couple of years, though. We would climb up the mountains to the woods where the charcoal burners used to burn the sticks. If there was nobody about—for instance, if the burners had gone down with a load of charcoal—then we'd go up to where they'd been burning and poke about in the earth with sticks to find any scraps of charcoal they might have left. You could always tell where they'd been burning the charcoal, because the earth was all soft and crumbly. We might pick up as much as ten to fifteen kilos each. When there wasn't any charcoal to be found, we would go down to the railway line and hunt for bits of coal and clinker along the track. We might pick up fifteen to twenty kilos each down there, too. An engine always drops some coal on the track as it goes along. And sometimes when a train's standing in the station, the stoker shovels out all the hard coal and clinker, and all the stony stuff that's no good to him. But the clinker's just the thing for tinsmiths, because it makes no smoke. Any good coal we picked up, we sold to blacksmiths: they have to have the best coal as it gives off the most heat.

These last few years, we've been going out to collect lead. The police practise target shooting over there—listen, can't you hear them pinging away now? They're always at it, the whole of May, all day long from morning till evening. Just throwing money away, when there's none to spare for us unemployed. You find a few bits of lead lying around on top, but mostly you have to dig for it, because the bullets go right into the ground. There must be heaps there, but of course we can't find them all. Sometimes they fire off several rounds at once—forty at one go, even. First, we look and see where they've made holes: those ones are easy to spot. Then we line out on the range and go over it all carefully, inch by inch, with our hoes. We pick up the little bits of aluminium, as well, from the casing of hand-grenades. And sometimes we find a live bullet or two that they've overlooked. Then of course we go and sell whatever we've collected.

And that's all the help we ever get from the authorities!

If you've got to earn your living with bullets, at least ours is a decent harmless way of doing it!

# Granny Nedda

YES, of course a husband's got the right to beat his wife. If she's given him cause to punish her, of course he's got the right. Say she starts arguing with him, answering him back—naturally, he won't stand for that, so he beats her. But for a wife to raise her hand against her husband—we won't hear of such a thing, it's disgraceful. 'Dragged up, that's what she was!' we say, if a woman does that. But if our husbands take the stick to us when we've done something wrong, well, that's as it should be.

If a woman gets beaten by her husband, the rest of us say: 'Well, he can't have beat her for nothing—there must have been good reason.' So of course we take his side. If a woman raises her hand against her husband, though, it's shameful: it shows she's a bad sort, a loose woman. A mare—that's what we call that kind of woman.

All wives get beaten from time to time, and that's only right and proper. It's only the bad ones, the mares, who go and complain. I ask you—is it right for a woman to speak ill of her husband just because he gives her a thrashing? A decent woman won't say a word about it to anyone. Take my granddaughter Saridda, now: the other day her husband gave her such a beating that her eyes were black and blue. 'Whoever did that to you?' I asked: 'How ever did you get those black eyes?' 'I fell down the steps, Granny,' she says—just like that! 'Fell down the steps!' I says—'And you just about to have a baby!' (She was expecting it any minute.) 'It's all right, Granny,' she says, 'it didn't do the baby any harm.' That's how a decent girl behaves. She won't tell anyone her husband hit her—not even her own mother.

Once, my husband gave me such a beating that he broke one of my ribs—it hurt so much I could hardly move, I had to go down on my knees to make the bed. But did I tell anyone?

When people asked me what was wrong, I said: 'It's nothing, it's just a headache.'

When a woman has been neglecting her duties as a wife, the neighbours get together, five or six of them maybe, and start picking her to pieces. 'What a dirty slut she is!' one of them will say: 'She's no use at anything—she can't even keep her house clean . . .' 'Why can't she ever wash her things? Her clothes are always filthy . . .' 'Why doesn't she get on with the housework, instead of standing about gossiping all day and speaking ill of honest folk behind their backs . . .' 'Her husband's quite right to beat her—look how she leaves her children crying at home while she stands about tittle-tattling in the street. . .' and so on. No, we've no use for a woman like that!

We women do enjoy a good chat, though. It makes a nice change—gives us something to think about. When the sun comes out, we go outside too and sit in the sun. 'Look!' they say, 'the sun's come out for a gossip!' And I always say: 'Well, and why shouldn't he?' It's so nice sitting out in the sun—you can breathe better. We talk about this and that, we get to know what everyone's doing and thinking. When the sun comes out, it means folk can go out and sit in the street and chat.

A wife who wants to keep her husband happy and contented must stay at home, and cook his meals for him, and keep the house clean and tidy, and wash and mend his clothes, and never deny him his rights, and never so much as look at another man. It's the husband who's master—master of the house, and her master too. Everything belongs to him, except the dowry linen. A husband has to be firm with his wife, he has to keep her on a tight rein, otherwise—who knows how she'd end up?

Well, now you know how things are in these parts: that's how husbands treat their wives around here. Perhaps it's different in other places—what do the Americans do, for instance? How do the Russians treat their wives? (The Russians —they're the ones with the red faces, aren't they?) And I've heard of some called the French, too . . .

When our husbands take the stick to us, they put us in the corner, and we just take whatever comes. We only have one husband, like we only have one God: 'One God—one husband,' the saying goes. And we take whatever he gives us, kisses or thrashings. We can't go out of the house, either, unless he says so: it's up to him to give the orders and decide everything. He's the master.

How did my mother die? I'll tell you. I heard the story from my sisters—I don't remember myself, as I was only a baby at the breast when it happened. One day, when she'd just been baking some bread, she got a blinding headache, and so she took a pillow and lay down on the settle. After a while my father (God rest him) came in, a little bit drunk. 'Rosalia,' he says to her, 'I want my bed brought out—get up!' 'I can't do it just now,' she says, 'my head's too bad, but call your daughter and get her to fetch the mattress and made the bed up for you.' So he called my sister and asked her to do it. But she answered him back: 'Why should I!' she said: 'You've just been wasting all our money on drink!' She was cross with him because she was hungry and he hadn't brought us back anything to eat. (This didn't happen often, though—mostly he was a good father to us.) Anyway, when my sister refused to fetch the mattress, he turned to my mother again and said: 'You'll have to make up my bed yourself, since your daughter won't.' But she said: 'I can't do it—I can't even hold my head up.' Then my father got mad, and grabbed her, and gave her such a clout on the head that it broke her jaws, and her teeth got wedged together so that she couldn't open her mouth. He didn't mean to, of course, but he was a bit drunk, and he didn't realise how hard he was hitting her. He was a strong man—a blacksmith, he was. They ran to fetch my godfather, who was a barber and knew a bit about doctoring people, and he tried to force her mouth open with a spoon—but it was too late. She was dead.

If a man falls ill, his wife prays to our Holy Mother to cure him, and makes all sorts of vows. Sometimes a wife will pray: 'Holy Mary, leave me my husband and take one of my sons instead.' If she thinks her man's going to die, she makes a solemn promise to the Virgin: 'Blessed Lady,' she says, 'if you'll cure my husband, I'll go down on my face in the church and lick all the stones from the church door right up to your altar.'

Then if the man gets well again, the wife carries out her vow on the next Feast day. She walks to the church bare-footed, and as soon as she gets to the door she goes down on her hands and knees and begins to crawl towards the altar, licking all the stones as she goes, licking up all the spit and dust and mud and filth, as a special devotion. The church is always crowded with people—walking about, spitting, the little ones doing wee-wee on the floor. 'Make way! Make way!' the people say: 'She's come to church to thank the Madonna!' and they all cry as they watch her. My daughter-in-law did it once.

When the woman's mouth is so sore and numb that she has to stop for a bit, she raises her head and cries out: 'Blessed Mother, thank you!' and then she crawls on again, licking and licking. Then when she gets to the altar at last, she stands up, and lifts up her arms, and thanks the Madonna with all her heart —praising her and thanking her for her mercies out loud so that everyone can hear, and with the tears streaming down her face. And all the people round her are weeping too—men as well as women, young and old alike. Then when it's over, she wets a handkerchief and wipes her tongue, which is all cracked and skinned and bleeding, and dries her eyes. They do this penance over at Romitello, too, and at Tagliavia. It's mostly young people who make this vow to lick the stones—perhaps the old folk are more resigned. In the old days, though, people never used to do this at all—it's only caught on in the last five years.

I've had my full share of sorrows—five little ones, the Lord has taken from me. One of them got the whooping-cough. He was only three when he died—I was still giving him the breast. My other son here, the one who's just got married—I suckled him for four years. They seemed such pitiful little things I never liked to wean them! This one used to come up to me while I was sewing and ask for it: 'Ma!' he'd say, 'Titty, Mamma!' so I'd let him suck away while I went on sewing.

But I was telling you about my little son who died. One day he was playing horses with a little boy who had the whooping-

cough, and he put the reins in his mouth and so he caught it too.
He was such a pretty little thing, small and delicate looking, a
bit like my grandson Fifiddu. He had fair hair, too—he took
after my husband's side of the family: my father-in-law was
quite fair. Carmeluzzu was my little boy's name.

Well, he caught the whooping-cough. I tell you, whenever
any of my children were ill . . . This one was so delicate I was
afraid he might die with the cough, so I went to the chemist's
and said: 'My little boy's got the whooping-cough—can I
please have some syrup to clear his chest?' So he made up some
syrup, and told me to give the boy a teaspoonful every half
hour. But it turned out he only took the one teaspoonful. When
I took him in my arms to give it him, he wouldn't touch it at
first. 'But it'll take away your cough, I promise.' Then I pretended to drink it myself: 'Look, you see, Mamma's having
some too!' and in the end I coaxed him into swallowing it.

Well, very soon after, he started having these terrible pains
in his tummy—but of course I had no idea what was wrong with
him. He started howling and screaming, and swearing like
anything, poor little soul: it was the medicine burning him up
inside, but I couldn't understand it at the time. It went on all
that day, and then all night.

I didn't know this till afterwards, either—but my little girl of
five secretly tasted some of the syrup too, because she thought
it would be nice and sweet (you know how children are with
sweet things), and of course she started having the pains too.

In the night, seeing Carmeluzzu was completely worn out,
every time he cried I gave him the breast to comfort him. The
next day, he was worse. In the evening when I tried to give him
the breast again, he wouldn't suck—he just turned his little
head away and stared up at the top of the bed. I was so exhausted
myself that I fell asleep.

On the third day, he died. In the morning, the young lady who
used to pay me to walk with her to the convent came to the door
and said: 'Are you ready, Donna Nedda?' But I said: 'I'm
afraid I can't come today, Signorina: my little boy's dreadfully
ill, I'm afraid he's dying.' She came right into the house then,

the young lady, to have a look at him; and when she saw him, she started to cry herself. In the end I did go with her, but only a little bit of the way—I came back as soon as I could, I ran all the way, and I picked up Carmeluzzu and tried to suckle him again. But I couldn't make him take it. Then I thought I'd give him a spoonful of water to freshen his poor little mouth. But when I put it in his mouth, he didn't swallow, the water stayed there in his throat, so I tipped his face down to let it run out again. How could he swallow it, poor little thing? He was dead. His little body was still warm.

I was all alone in the house. I just sat there, sobbing: 'My son, my son,' holding him in my arms. Then my daughter Ciccina came in, and I said: 'Look, your little brother's dead!' I couldn't stop crying. Then we dressed him, and my neighbour gave me a beautiful blue ribbon for him, and Ciccina went out to buy him a little pair of white socks.

They made out the death certificate at once, as fast as they could. When I think of it . . . In less than an hour, they'd been and taken him away. As soon as the chemist who'd given me the syrup heard Carmeluzzu was dead, he asked the man who owns the carriages, who happened to be a friend of his, to come and take the body away at once. They were anxious to get him away quickly, you see, before anyone else found out about it.

By this time my little girl was taken ill too—her insides were turning to water. 'I couldn't cry for Carmeluzzu,' she told me, 'because I thought I was dying too.' She confessed that she'd tasted some of the medicine herself. As soon as she said that, my eldest son picked up the glass it was in and flung it out of the house, and I snatched up my little girl and ran down to the other chemist's near the fish market. 'Quick!' I said. 'She took some cough syrup and it's made her ill—do something for her, please!' I was sure she was dying too. He led me into a room at the back, and while I held her in my arms, he examined her all over and felt her poor little tummy, and then he gave her some medicine. 'Are you the mother of the little boy who was poisoned?' he asked me. 'Poisoned?' I said. I didn't understand then. But it seems that the man who made up the syrup in the first chemist's was a beginner—he didn't know his job properly, and he must have mixed in something from one of those little bottles with the death's head on.

Anyway, this other chemist gave my little girl a purge to clear out her insides. 'I'll be good and take the medicine,' she said: she understood, you see, she knew she had to take it to make her well again. The next few days, I wouldn't let her have anything to eat—I kept her on milk.

About a week later, a man came to see my husband. 'Listen, Peppino,' he said: 'I won't go on about this business—it's quite bad enough for you as it is. But I just want to advise you to let the matter drop. It's no good making a fuss—you're poor and they're rich, so they're bound to win. Just think, Peppino—what's the use? If you go and get the little boy's body dug up again, it's you who'll have to pay all the costs. And they'll win in the end, whatever happens—they're rich. Take my advice, and just give it up.'

# Leonardo, a young shepherd

WHAT did I do all day when I was little? I played in the road-way! When I was thirteen, I took a job as a shepherd. My father's a shepherd, and I learnt first by helping him with his sheep. After you've been tending them for a year, you know all about them.

In the early days, my father used to tend the flocks on his own, but soon I joined him and helped him look after the young ones. When I was at San Giorgio, they didn't want me to milk the ewes—but I milked them all the same, because I liked doing it. If you squeeze their teats too hard the first time you milk them, they never forget, and they won't let you milk them any more. And you must be careful, too, not to scratch their udders with your nails. They're all different to milk, you know. Some of them'll stand quite quietly, but others are not so tame, and they kick out at you. With some, the milk comes easily, but with others it's much harder. Some have proper straight teats, but others are crooked. There are some people that animals can't stand—they won't let them come near. But they always let me handle them.

I can't count, but even from quite a distance I can tell just by looking if one of my sheep or goats is missing. I can tell them all apart. Even in a big flock, I know every one by sight, and which lamb or kid belongs to which mother. I've had flocks of as many as a hundred or two hundred sheep. The owner used to count them to see if they were all there, but I could tell without counting, just by looking.

I love my sheep, and they love me. I look after them well, and follow them wherever they go, and stroke them and pet them and pick little beans to feed them on; and they're so tame with me they come right up to me.

They don't have names, but I only have to shout and they all turn round. I can tell when a ewe's going to lamb because her udder gets all swollen and she stops eating. When the labour starts, she lies down on the ground and begins to bleat, and the waters break. If it goes all right, she soon stops bleating; but if I see she can't manage by herself, then I go and help her, and make the opening bigger with my hands. The lamb's forefeet come first, and then its face. Then the minute it's born, the mother starts licking it clean and drying it. As soon as that's finished, she gets up, and after about a quarter of an hour or half an hour the lamb stands up too and begins to suck. The first time I watched a lamb being born was with my father—it was by helping him that I learnt how to deal with the lambing.

We call the young ewes *renische*: they're not called *pecore* till after they've lambed. The young nanny-goats are called *ciaravedde,* and the ones that have only had one kid are *primarole*. After that they're all just called goats.

Young kids aren't the same as lambs: we have to keep them penned in, separated from their mothers, for the first month. If they're allowed to follow the mother about when they're tiny, they get much too thin and scraggy. Of course they want to go after the mothers, and they're always trying to escape: but they're only supposed to see them twice a day, morning and evening, for suckling. Otherwise they'd get too skinny. After the first month, though, they are allowed out—the ones you've decided to rear, that is: the others are slaughtered. By that time the navel cords will have shrivelled up and dropped off by themselves.

They're nice creatures, sheep and goats. I always take them where the grass is juiciest. If they can't find anything to eat, you should just hear them bleating! When the sun's blazing down at midday they all huddle up together and try to get into each other's shadows; then later in the afternoon they wander off in all directions.

The only places I've been to are Castellana and Alimena. I don't understand anything about money.

There's a plant we call '*daps*' and if sheep nibble even a tiny bit of it they die at once: so what you do always is to let the goats in first to eat up the flowers. It doesn't poison them, you see—

it's quite harmless to goats. After that, it doesn't matter if the sheep 'eat the rest of the plant, as it's only the flower that's poisonous to them.

Sometimes, to pass the time, I make a little figure out of clay, and then I set it up and throw stones at it and try to knock it down. You have to do something to pass the time. Some shepherds have little pipes and play tunes on them. I haven't got a pipe, though—I wouldn't know how to make one. But I can make these clay dolls. Or sometimes I pile stones up one on top of the other, and throw pebbles at them to knock them down again. I could hit one as far away as the road there. That's a game all shepherds play.

Stars? I've seen them often enough, but I don't know what they are. You see them in those little pictures of Jesus, too. Perhaps they're some sort of eyes, the stars—I've no idea what they are. But the moon is the Madonna. I've heard people say that the moon's the Madonna, and I think they're right: the moon is the Madonna, and the sun is Our Lord. I pray to them. When it's cold, I pray to the sun to come out and warm me; and when it's too hot, I pray to him to make it a bit cooler. When it's dark, I pray to the moon to come out and shine for me.

I love the sun and the moon. When it's cold, the sun comes out and makes me nice and warm. And when it's dark, the moon comes out and lights my way so that I can see where I'm going. Sometimes I pray to the stars as well: 'Please shine for me,' I say. I love watching the stars—they're beautiful.

What I like best is when I have a holiday—I go back home to my village for the day, and I see my mother and my brothers and my father, and all my uncles. But I like being with my animals, too. I like working. I'd like to be a proper farmer though, and sow and reap, and be able to eat as much as I wanted.

Sometimes I pray for fine weather; or I pray that it won't rain, in winter, and that there won't be any thunderstorms. I pray to Our Lord: 'Oh, dear kind Father,' I say to him out loud: 'don't let there be bad weather!' It's the wind that makes it cold. What is the wind? Well, the grass blows about—you see it swaying this way and that—and that's the wind. If it's cold, you pray to the sun to make it warm again, as it's better for the animals when it's warm. It was my mother who taught me to pray to the sun—her and my father. Us shepherds always pray to the sun to warm us, and to the moon to give us light at night.

The sea? Yes, I've heard of the sea, but I don't know what it is. I've always lived up here, summer and winter, so I've never seen it. But I think the world's a sea—at least, that's what I've heard. 'The world's a sea of troubles,' they say.

I see the clouds, but I don't know what they are. When the wind blows they go away.

What are we in the world for? Well, because that's where we live, and work. And eat. We're here to work. To eat. To work —I don't know!

Men grow old, everything in the world grows old, human beings and animals alike. Only the sun never grows old.

# Crocifissa, in her house on the landslide

SIT down, please. Don't be afraid—it's not going to move today. Tonight, though, God only knows ...

Three times, we've had to leave this house because of the landslide. With official notice to quit each time. It started in '35. At first, it was just a few cracks in the earth floor. Then the walls began to crack too, and we couldn't shut the door any more because the walls had settled—the whole house was shifting. The week before my daughter Pina was born, the whole floor came up in a hump, and one wall started to split and crumble. Then the roof began to sag down. It wasn't only this house—the same thing was happening to all the other houses round: walls bulging out or caving in, leaning all over the place. It was winter then, and I had three young children, so we had to leave the house and take refuge with my father.

We appealed to the Council, and they sent along an engineer. He inspected the landslide, and had us all turned out at once— he gave us notice to quit immediately because of course he didn't want to be responsible if anything happened. The whole quarter was shifting, every house was damaged.

In June, we started to repair the house. Then in September, since we couldn't possibly find the money to get a house somewhere else, we moved back.

But in 1940 it started to move again: the floor split and folded up, and a whole chunk of wall fell down. By this time I had four children—I was glad about that, I'd been wanting another as three didn't seem enough. In February, we got another order to quit. The engineers came along again, and said they wouldn't be answerable for the consequences if we stayed. So in March we moved out, this time into another house which we rented. We hadn't been there long, though, when my husband died; so I was left with the four children, and just had to manage as best I could. I drew the insurance money, and with that and the bit of money I'd managed to save before, I had the house repaired; and by September we were back living in it again.

But every year since then, whenever it rains heavily, a bit more damage is done: in a dry year, of course, it's not so bad. As there's nowhere else we can go, we just have to stay on here. They keep turning us out, but we have to come back again. Every year the houses slip a little further, inch by inch. They've moved over two yards now since the landslide started. The houses higher up press down on the ones below, and they're all slowly but surely sliding down the hill. And as the houses move, the electric cables snap, and the lights go: we've often been suddenly plunged in darkness. The streets are all breaking up, too. And from time to time the drains burst—where they're lucky enough to have drains, that is. Great chunks of stone and plaster come tumbling down—and sometimes a whole house collapses.

We sow the fields in springtime, but mostly the crops never come up: the earth cracks and crumbles and slithers away down the hillside.

The water pipes burst too, of course—they've burst over at Zu Vincenzo's, for instance, and all over the place. Things don't generally happen all of a sudden, though: usually we can tell when danger's coming, and have time to get out of the house. But sometimes it happens at night. Last year when my son was here he woke up in the night to find pieces of mortar falling down on top of him—he had to jump up and rush outside.

Our animals always know when something's going to happen. They snuff around and get very restless, and start stamping and pawing the ground—they can always tell when there's danger in the air. One night—back in 1940, this was—I was woken up all of a sudden by the sound of the mules stamping and pawing the ground. Bits of plaster had begun to fall, and we just had time to escape into the open. The minute the animals hear the stones beginning to fall, they get scared and try to escape: it's a dreadful thing, violent death, and we're all terrified of it—animals as well as humans.

We're on a kind of bush-telegraph in these houses—a thief wouldn't stand a chance! We can hear everything that's going on in each other's houses through the cracks in the walls. If we want to have a private conversation, we have to whisper. And it's not just a matter of being overheard—you can see through the cracks, too. I hardly need to have the light on in here at night—I can see quite well by the light from next door shining through the cracks. You have to turn your light out before you get undressed at night, otherwise the people in the next door houses can see you. Sometimes when you're just sitting down to a meal—crash! down comes a lump of plaster from the ceiling and you find you're eating rubble with your supper.

When it's windy, you can feel the house shaking and trembling all over, like someone with a fever. If there's a gale, it's safer to go out into the open. But sometimes we're so frightened we just bury our heads and trust to God. Sometimes at night when there's a strong wind shaking the walls, we sit in here and pray to Saint Rosalia to make the wind drop.

We get all the smoke from each other's fires seeping through the cracks in the walls, too. We're always having the cracks filled in, but in no time at all they open up again.

Once upon a time, we had this whole floor quite level and smooth, but now look at it! You can hardly stand a chair upright—you'd think you were up on the mountain side! Two years ago, I had the whole place done up properly all over again: the kitchen put to rights, the floor levelled, the walls mended—everything. But soon another crack appeared, and before long another lump of plaster fell down . . . and now we're back where we started. Since March, I've been under notice to quit again, and so are the six other families who've stayed here. Every year, more people move away.

You can see the landslide, over there. There's a rocky mountain above us called the Ilice. Before, the stream used to run out over by Totò Battaglia's place: but then they built a wall there and cut it off, so that instead of running away through the fields, the water comes right over this way and ruins our houses. The stream's got no proper bed now, you see, it's got no outlet, so when there's been a lot of rain it spreads and runs all over the place. And of course, since we're just underneath, most of it runs straight down here. What they ought to do of course is to channel it away before it ever gets this far.

There are about two hundred and forty houses affected by the landslide—just about the whole Santa Rosalia quarter. The water's been sucking away at the earth, sucking away at the foundations, and the houses are tottering. The whole quarter is sliding, the whole mountainside is slipping and sliding down. The people are angry, they go and protest to the Council, but of course the Council are too busy looking after their own interests. So the landslide goes on getting worse and worse. And meanwhile poor men with families to support are ruining themselves trying to keep up with repairing the damage.

Whenever we go to the Council to try and get them to do something about it—to halt the landslide, in the first place, and then to give us some help in repairing the houses—it's always the same story: 'Yes, of course. We'll start work on it at once —today, tomorrow . . .' But a fat lot they care! Just before the elections, they come round handing out keys: 'Here you are, this is for you: it's the key to the new house we've found you.' But the rest of the time, it's just: 'Your house isn't safe—you'll have to leave.'

'But where are we to go?' we ask.

'You'll just have to find somewhere else,' they say. What do they expect us to do—camp out?

The engineers and the other authorities come along. 'You poor things!' they say pityingly; and if the house is in danger of falling, they tell us: 'You can't stay here.' But as for finding us anywhere else to go . . .

'We'll be starting the repair work on Monday,' they say: 'Your houses will be fixed next month . . .' As for doing something about the landslide—'The Council's very short of funds,' they tell us: 'We've none to spare, in fact we're in debt already.' But really they're only interested in their own affairs.

My son can only find work two or three months in the year. We very poor people are so ignorant about everything, we've no idea what's going on in the world. We hardly ever see a newspaper—it's only the well-to-do who can afford to read the papers. But occasionally if there's some very important news— a big disaster, say, or if we hear from the shopkeepers that something specially interesting's happened—then one or two people in the district may buy a paper. Someone'll come along and call us: 'Tizia's bought a paper!' and we all go along to her house and sit round listening while somebody reads aloud. I also hear bits of news from time to time from a relation of mine who lives in Palermo: 'So-and-so's quarrelled with his wife,' she tells me, or: 'So-and-so's killed himself jumping out of a train.'

There are at least twenty-seven people here who've been driven out of their minds by fear, or by hunger and weakness. Only last week—Saturday, it was—a woman ran away up the Ilice mountain there and threw herself over the edge. She'd gone crazy with fear. Half her wall had caved in on her and she'd been left clinging to the window ledge. She was so terrified she went out of her mind and killed herself. Then there's a man in the next street who screams and screams, then stops for an hour or two, then starts screaming again. Sometimes he shouts the most terrible things: 'He must die! He must die! You've eaten human flesh!' He used to be such a good worker, too. He screams and screams, and the neighbours are trying to have him certified and put away.

Every so often, we're woken up in the midde of the night by someone shouting, and we all jump up in a fright and rush outside, with our faces as white as plaster.

The beams work loose from the walls and come toppling down. We've forgotten what it's like to be free from fear— from one minute to the next we know we may be crushed and killed.

On the eve of Saint Joseph's day, a whole house collapsed, just four doors down from here. It was terrible. Tano's little girl was out there in the street, and the stones suddenly started tumbling down, and people shouted to her: 'Look out! the house is falling down! The house is falling down!' The cat flew out, and cr-r-r-ash! the whole house collapsed, just like that —and the child was still standing there screaming.

Our doorways keep getting narrower and narrower all the time. When we can't shut them any more, we call in the carpenter, but still they go on getting narrower and narrower. This one's shrunk a hand's breadth already. The other night I dreamt our door was so narrow that the only way I could get out was through the window. If only it *was* all a dream! Sometimes you can actually hear the walls scrunching as they bulge out. At night, you're woken by the thud of a falling brick. You turn on the light and look around, then you turn it off again and go back to sleep. A little later, though, another thud . . . this may happen two or three times in one night.

In winter, we hardly sleep at all. The rainwater streams down, the houses begin to slide—everything begins to slide. The people all go along and protest, but the Council are too busy looking after their own interests. Once, a man who could write came round and collected six hundred lire from each of us and had some complaints drawn up for us. But nothing ever came of that—we never heard anything more about it.

Then we all signed our names to another petition, which we sent to the Chief of Police, the Regional Assembly, and the Government. A few months ago, the Honourable F. came to Alia. He took a look round, and then declared that the landslide didn't exist! Then Antonino and some of the other men got this letter—I've got a copy, I'll show you . . .

REPUBLIC OF ITALY, REGION OF SICILY
THE PRESIDENT

A.E.L. DIVISION 111, ref. 22/589                    Palermo,
                                                    26. 10. 55.

To: Mr. Todaro Antonino fu Francesco
Via Savoia,
Alia.

Dear Sir,
     With reference to your request for aid, we wish to state

that we have been in communication with the technical experts concerned regarding the displacements of soil observed in Via Gorizia of the Commune of Alia, and have now been informed that the said displacements do not appear to constitute a true landslide. Since the reported damage is not, therefore, the consequence of a natural disaster, no claim for State Assistance can be entertained.

(signed) Deputy Assessor.

# Gino: the story of an ex-pick-pocket

I'LL TELL you how my life began. My mother was a widow—her husband had been a shoemaker by trade. Since she worked as a *spicciafaccende*,[1] she was in and out of the Town Hall a lot, and it was there she met my father, who worked in one of the offices. She was a real good-looker, and he took a fancy to her, and he soon got his way with her by promising to marry her. Of course what he didn't tell her was that he was married already!

I was born in 1912, a bastard. My mother couldn't bring herself to part with me, and as I hadn't a name legally, she gave me hers. I don't remember much about those early days. I only remember playing out in the street; and I've also a dim recollection of being left in the care of a neighbour while my mother went out to work. But that's all.

When the Spanish 'flu epidemic hit Sicily, my mother caught it and died. No one turned up; her family had written her off because she'd gone wrong, and as I was a child of sin no one wanted to have anything to do with me.

However, I had a grown up half-brother who was engaged, and in the end I was taken in by his girl's family. There was a young pick-pocket living in the house, and before long he started to teach me the tricks of the trade. He began by showing me how to open, or 'flap', a woman's handbag—a *magghia appendente*, a 'trawling net', it's called in thieves' slang. He taught me how to do it by the *frontino* and *mezzo frontino* way. I'll explain: *frontino* means from the front. What I had to do was to walk along five or six yards in front of the victim, then turn round sharply so that I was face to face with her. As soon as I came about level with her handbag, passing her on the side she was holding it, I'd lift up the arm nearest her so I could get at the bag under cover of my own elbow, and quick as a flash I'd un-

[1] See Old Andrea's account of the life of the *spicciafaccende*, page 108.

fasten the bag. I had to be able to deal with every kind of fastening—buttons were common in those days, but there were all sorts of clasps too, and even zips: you had to be expert at them all. Then the minute you'd opened the bag you turned half round—*mezzo frontino*—and slipped your hand in and nicked the wallet, or whatever else was in there.

Once a kid had learnt the trade, his problem was to convince people he could be trusted and get someone to take him on. After a bit, some chap who'd been a pick-pocket himself in his young days might get to hear about him. 'There's a kid who knows his job and who won't split,' he'd say to himself, and so he'd go along and hire him. Then the pair of them would travel all over the place and work every city in Italy.

My first master was a certain B. I'll never forget the first time I went out with him. I was in such a panic I wet my pants—I was scared stiff the woman would see what I was up to and clout me one. If I hadn't been still more scared that B. would call me yellow and give me the chuck, I'd never have gone through with it. I've known some kids who used to screw up their courage and steady their nerves with drink or drugs. After that first time, though, it wasn't so bad. B. used always to give a proportion of our takings to his family for my keep—I was lodging with them. I never saw the money myself: it was always him who opened the wallets, and he never gave me the satisfaction of knowing how much was in them. I usually managed to pinch two or three a day. His part was to play the *palo*, or 'post', which means standing in the way so as to make sure passers by won't see what's going on.

In the street I lived in, almost every family had a youngster like myself learning to be a pick-pocket. Via Sant'Agostino, Cortile Catarro, Cortile Salaro—practically every street in the neighbourhood had either its fully-fledged pick-pocket or else its 'college' for student pick-pockets. It's just the same today— there's hundreds of young pick-pockets down there, and at Ballarò, and all over the place. Via Montalbo, Via Castro, Rione Borgo—half Palermo's swarming with them! Some of the 'graduates' from here even emigrate to America, and there are lots who go to the big Italian cities—Turin, Milan, Genoa. Up there they won't be recognised, and they find things much easier than here. The people up there aren't familiar with their tricks, so picking their pockets is child's play. They do quite well in Rome, too, because the prostitutes there are willing to help them in the *nona* trick—that is, making up to a chap to distract him while they're picking his pockets. But I'd better not tell you too much—I don't want to give everything away and see the thieves all rounded up and hauled off to prison! The authorities wouldn't dream of trying to help them live a better life by finding them some honest work to do instead, so of course they come out of prison worse than when they went in. We don't want a repetition of what happened that time Prefect Mori was sent here to clean things up—it was crazy, they were putting absolutely everybody in prison. In fact, though, the effect of that was that a lot of us got away with it altogether: in this quarter, at least, if somebody spotted one of us on the job they didn't say anything—they knew what it would mean for us if they did. Even the shopkeepers kept mum and didn't raise the alarm, and so we could be sure of escaping even when someone had witnessed the operation!

They still have squads of so-called 'special' police patrolling the city on the look-out for pick-pockets—but in fact nowadays there's nothing so very special about them. In my time, though, there were some famous squads—Sciàbbica's, for instance: he was a holy terror, Sciàbbica was. He's retired now, but sleuthing's in his blood: he can't live without it, and so he still does a bit on his own account. There was another famous squad chief we used to call 'Lu Signorino', because he smarmed his hair down with brilliantine. Sciàbbica was a terror, though. He could run like a hare.

One day—I'll never forget it—I was 'going down' (which means going to 'work') with my gang, when all of a sudden, on the corner of Via Sant'Agostino and Via Maqueda (this was the favourite spot for pick-pockets because people doing their shopping and lingering to look in the windows are an easy prey)—all of a sudden, I spotted Sciàbbica and his squad. 'Run for it! Sciàbbica!' I said, and we instantly turned and scattered and hared for dear life up the side alleys. I belted home—I never stopped running till I got inside the house. My sides were splitting, I was gasping for breath, but I didn't dare slacken speed—I knew if I was copped I'd be held in jail for at least three days. I was in a real panic at the thought that they might have spotted me. It's always an anxious moment for the folk at home when you arrive back in that state—they never know whether you've just grabbed a wallet and made a dash for it, or whether you've been spotted and the cops are on to you. They just have to stand round in suspense till you get your breath back enough to explain what's happened! Alarms, panic, flight, thrills, constant fear of running into the police squads—that's the life of the pick-pockets. Every morning when a gang sets out to work, they know the squads are setting out too.

So far, I've only been telling you about the pick-pockets who steal from *minule*—women, that is. There are other gangs who specialise in robbing a *vascu*, a man. These ones use a dodge known as the *sciammaru*, which gets its name from the type of short jacket men wear. One of the team has to be just the right height—that's to say, he has to be able to brush aside the man's jacket unobtrusively with his elbow as he passes. They usually have a kid aged about twelve to fifteen to do this bit. As he walks past, the lad brushes the victim's jacket aside so that his accomplice coming along just behind can see whether the wallet—*u surci*, the 'mouse', as it's called in thieves' slang—is in the man's right or left hand pocket. As soon as the one behind sees which side it's on, he lets the lad in front know by putting either his right or his left hand on the lad's shoulder. The lad then brushes the jacket to one side again, this time on the side where he knows the 'mouse' is, and so his accomplice can slip in his hand easily and pinch it.

This operation's really quite easy if the man happens to find himself in the midst of a spot of confusion—which of course is generally created to order by the gang or some of their accomplices. It may be a carriage driving by that just misses knocking him down, or a bicycle skimming past him; or he may

F

find himself in the middle of quite a little crowd. Usually there'll be about four or five of these hustlers in the team. You know how old tarts go on scraping some sort of a living by washing down steps in the district where they've been selling themselves for, maybe, twenty years or so—well, these hustlers are doing the same sort of thing: they're the old lags who've had more than enough of prison and prefer to do the less risky part of the business. They do the *palo*, for instance—the 'post', that is, when they stand there and block the view from passers by— and all the other little tricks. There's the *nona*, too, when they distract a man by bumping into him from in front, or else by taking his shoulders from behind and pushing past him as if they're in a hurry to overtake him. If the gang succeed in nabbing the wallet, whatever money they get is shared out among them. Half of it is split between the young lad and the bloke who actually pinched the 'mouse', and the rest of the gang are paid according to what part they've played. The *nona* gets least—whatever the rest of them choose to give him: he's not really considered one of the gang, he's just what you might call a casual.

Most of the victims are country people who've come down to Palermo to go to hospital, or to look for work, or to do their shopping: they always bring all their savings with them. Pick-pockets also keep a sharp look out for *fardaioli*, emigrants who've been working in the States or in South America for years and have just come back to Sicily: these types are pretty well certain to have a *surciu abbuzzatu*, a wallet stuffed with notes.

Pick-pockets aren't the only ones who prey on these people —there are all sorts of other tricksters after them too. For instance, you get the type who can pass himself off as an American. He rigs himself out in the blue jersey and the cap with the anchor on, and makes out he's just come off the boat. '*Scusare, Consolato Americano?*' he'll say to some innocent; and then he'll start talking about the real good 'English' stuff in his case that he wants to sell. It ends up, of course, with him unloading a whole lot of rubbish on the poor fool! Then there are the pick-pockets who specialise in robbing people on buses—because a pick-pocket has to specialise, you know: each sort of job is quite different. On buses the difficult thing, especially in winter, is to get at the trouser pockets underneath the coat.

By the time I was twelve, I'd made quite a name for myself as a pick-pocket. There was a kind of thieves' hiring market, and one day this bloke came along to see the family I was living with, and told them he'd like to take me on, and agreed to give them so much for me. And so I left home, and my new life began. I was on the up and up now.

We travelled around together, and my new boss even took me onto the mainland. What did we do? The same sort of thing as before. It makes me feel bad now just to think of the life I led then. One dodge we worked was the *appiccico*: my boss would stride along the street brandishing his belt, and I'd pretend to be running away from him. 'Has anyone seen my kid?' he'd ask passers by: 'He's run away from home, been missing three days—wait till I lay my hands on him, I'll tan his hide off!' The next minute he'd let out a shout. 'There he is!' he'd exclaim, pointing at me, and I'd dodge away with him after me. Then I'd throw myself down at the feet of the first man I spotted who looked as if he had a nice fat 'mouse' in his back pocket, and I'd clutch him round the knees and howl: 'Save me! Save me! Don't let my father beat me!' I'd cling to him for dear life as my 'father' raised the belt and began to slash at me, and while the kind gentleman was doing his best to protect me from the blows, the boss would neatly nick his wallet. As soon as he'd got his hands on it, he'd clear his throat to let me know the operation was completed, and I'd leave go of the man's legs and get up and go off, still sobbing and sniffling, with my 'father'.

We often used to hire a *carrozza* whose driver was in the know to come along behind us in case we had to make a quick getaway. Once on the Corso dei Mille, here in Palermo, near the Mulino Pecoraro, a man came past us carrying about ten empty bottles. Well, we saw our chance, and my boss at once went for his wallet—but just as he was extracting it from his pocket, the bloke spotted what we were up to. 'Excuse me,' he said to a passer by, 'my trousers are coming down—would you mind holding some of these a moment?' Then at once he pulled out a revolver and started firing at us. We were scared out of our wits—we flung ourselves into the *carrozza* and made off as fast as we could. The crowd hearing the shots thought it was just the usual story—they thought a girl had been kidnapped and someone was firing at her abductors.

Well, we travelled about for a while, mainly between Palermo and Naples. Usually we stayed in hotels—we wore decent suits and looked altogether respectable, and made out we were commercial travellers. We went to Milan, too, and Turin—all over the place. At one time my boss even managed to get hold of a Press card and posed as a journalist. Every so often we'd come back to Palermo, our base.

When I was fifteen, the authorities decided to send me to the Reformatory at Santa Maria Capua Vetere, in the province of Naples. I was put on the boat in the charge of a policeman— who of course had no idea that among the other passengers was a bloke I'd been working with who was determined that I shouldn't be put away. After we'd landed and the cop had seen me safely onto the train, my mate gave me some sort of mixture to rub in my eyes to make them red and inflamed so that when I got to the Reformatory they'd discharge me as unfit. As I couldn't bear the thought of losing my freedom— and by this time I'd got a real taste for travelling around Italy —I did what he suggested. And it worked: eight days later, I was discharged. However, to this day, I still suffer from conjunctivitis.

I went home for a bit, then, but before long I was off again, roaming from town to town all over Italy. Twice I was arrested and sentenced, the first time to twenty days, the second time to thirty: but although both sentences were recorded in my dossier, I didn't actually serve them, as I was still under age. Then one day in Rome I was arrested again. This time I was detained, and finally I was sent to the Vittorio Emanuele III Institute in the province of Mantua.

It was my time in that Reformatory that first made a rebel of me. They used to beat us for the least little thing. The Superintendent was a monster—he did things I can't repeat. If we so much as dared kick a ball around while he was having his afternoon nap, he'd give us two or three days in the cells. We used to creep down at night and pick the lock of the kitchen cupboard to pinch a bit of bread, or else we'd sneak out into the garden and steal melons and tomatoes. The Superintendent was terrible—I can't tell you . . . In the end, we decided to report him to the Mayor. We wrote a letter complaining of the outrages we'd had to suffer at his hands, and all the senior boys signed it. As luck would have it, it fell to me to deliver it to the Mayor! When I got back, the Superintendent was so mad he even threatened me with a revolver—but the Mayor investigated our complaints, and in the end the Superintendent was dismissed.

Three years, I spent in that Reformatory. It was like a prison —you can imagine the sort of life. Sometimes we used to sacrifice part of our bread ration to save up and swap with the local peasants for one or two of their home-made fags. It was a long, long walk to school, and all along the way people would look at us and say, in their funny dialect: 'Poor little devils —come on, let's give them a bit of bread and a drop of wine.'

Goodness knows what sort of teachers they were in that school. The first one seemed to believe in abandoning everything to the rule of anarchy; but the one who came after was a real dictator—or at least he tried to be, but in fact things generally turned out quite the opposite from what he intended. Anyway, we could never decide whether we were worse off under the first one or the second!

As I could read a bit, they started me off in the third class. I was just beginning to grow a beard, and I looked like the father of all the little village kids who were in the same class! I still remember my first day at school. The teacher chalked a triangle up on the blackboard and said: 'To find the area of this triangle, we multiply the base by the height and halve the answer . . .' He fixed his eye on me and said: 'You, boy, do you understand?' 'Yes sir,' I said—of course I hadn't the faintest idea what he was talking about! After that, we had Dictation: '*Oh little mare,* (comma) *little grey mare,*' he read; and I wrote '. . . *comma little grey mare.*' Then: '*You were good, but you cannot talk,* (full stop)'; and I wrote '. . . *full stop*'.

By the time I got up to the sixth Elementary class, I was eighteen. Then one day I was caught kissing the Mayor's niece in the garden near the school, and I was expelled on the spot. So there I was, turned out to face the world, without having learnt any skill whatever. All they'd taught me there in the way of a trade was a little bit about agriculture—but I ask you, what was the use of teaching that sort of thing to a city chap like me? What on earth did they expect me to do? Go and grow cucumbers in Saint Peter's Square?

The authorities found a foster-home for me in Rome. I lived there for three years, and during that time I learnt to be a barber. I hadn't forgotten my old friends, of course, but I wanted to make a new life for myself. Then, although I begged to be allowed to stay in Rome with my foster mother, the police there insisted on having me transferred back to Palermo. The police in Palermo didn't know what do do with me either, and in the end, after a lot of to-ing and fro-ing, they solved their problem by banishing me to the Island: two years of confinement on Pantelleria. I just can't tell you about the unspeakable things that went on there. It was one perpetual corruption. I ask you, was that the way to make a decent human being of a chap—was that the way?

I was twenty-two when I left Pantelleria. I didn't have to do my military service—I was rejected on account of the chronic conjunctivitis. I went straight back to Rome, and started to work as a barber again. I got customers, attended them in their own houses, made new friends, and lived a normal life. I'd reached a point where I realised I must break with my past once and for all. And I'd decided I wanted a family of my own, too: I felt a real need for love, and for responsibility. If a man doesn't have any feelings of responsibility—who knows where he'll end up?

Gradually, though, I grew more and more homesick for the city where I'd spent my childhood, and so before long I came back here to Palermo. But it was quite different for me now that I'd become a respectable citizen and started earning an honest living as a barber. Now I could enjoy a drink in the Caffè delle Rose, and saunter about at ease under the clock of the Massimo theatre, the favourite rendezvous of all the toffs and the bourgeoisie. When I went back to the Capo, the miserable quarter where I'd been born, I felt quite a stranger. Sometimes I'd bump into one of my old mates there. 'Listen,' I'd say: 'You may think it's a fine life, with the amount of easy money you can make and spend in a day: but you have to pay for it in the end—you'll pay for it with years in prison. I used to lie awake at night and shudder at the very thought of Sciàbbica, but all that's over and done with—I'm going straight now. If you've done an honest day's work, you go to bed with a quiet mind, and sleep soundly till morning.' But though I used to talk to them like this, I hadn't really solved the problem of my own future yet, or made any definite plans. I just had this feeling of great weariness and revulsion against all the misery I'd been through.

I very much wanted to get married and start a family, but I was only just making enough to live on myself—I couldn't put anything by. So one day I asked a friend of mine if he knew of any job going which would bring in a bit more; he said there might be one in a cement factory, and promised to put in a word for me in the right quarter. The 'right quarter' turned out to be a retired master-thief, a rascally old cripple, who unofficially controlled the whole factory from the outside—it was entirely up to him which chaps were hired and which were fired. I got taken on as a labourer, but the work was far too heavy for me. I toiled away like a beast of burden, stoking up the furnace, or carting loads of baked blocks around in an iron barrow. But I simply hadn't the strength for it, and three or four or five times a day I'd have to go to the latrine for a rest. Before long, of course, the old bully got to hear of this. 'There's no room here for a lazy bastard like you,' I was told—and that was that: I'd got the sack.

I did everything I could think of to try and earn the money I had to have before my girl and I could get married. I worked on commission, trying to get orders for wax figurines, selling all sorts of things—materials, 'gold' watches, and so on. I worked as a *spicciafaccende* for a bit, too. And I even tried my hand at ladies' hairdressing, though I wasn't much good at that! But try as I would, I still couldn't make enough money to put anything by. My girl couldn't see why we had to wait—she thought two could live as cheaply as one anyway—and in the end she got fed up and threatened to break it all off. I couldn't bear to lose her, or to think that all the sacrifices I'd made so far had been wasted, so in the end I asked her to run away with me. And so we ran away to Rome together: and there we were, without a place to live in, and me without even a job! Back in Palermo, people were saying: 'Poor little thing—she must have gone out of her mind. Fancy running away with a man who's got no work and can't possibly keep her!'

It was my foster mother in Rome who took us in: she'd always been a real comfort and strength to me. What little she had, she shared with us—and goodness knows she had little enough. We got married then, my girl and I—just a poor man's wedding of the simplest sort. But not long afterwards, my wife fell ill and had to go to hospital. I still hadn't been able to find a job, and things were going from bad to worse. Often I went to bed without any supper because there was no money. But what I minded most was having to go empty-handed to the hospital to visit my wife. I found it utterly humiliating—I felt I wasn't a real man, a proper husband. What a red-letter day it was when I was able to take her an orange. An *orange*! What's an orange? To me it was everything.

I felt desperately alone. I went round from barber's shop to barber's shop in the hope of finding one who'd take me on—but it was no use. Things reached such a pitch that I was tempted to get in touch with some of my old colleagues and take up the other line of business again—but I was held back by the fear that I'd be put inside again and so my wife would be left all on her own. One day, though, I accidentally ran into an old pick-pocketing mate of mine, and he gave me five lire. That kept me in food for two days, and it also meant that at last I could buy a present for my wife. But my mother realised the turn my thoughts had taken, and the struggle that was going on in my mind. One evening when I was sitting at the table with her eating my soup, she said to me: 'Now look, Gino love, you're not to do anything silly. Remember you've got a wife now, and you've got to look after her properly, specially as she's only a girl. I know what's in your mind—but you just can't do that sort of thing now.' Her good advice calmed me down and comforted me—and it seems it brought me luck, too, for a few days later I was taken on by a Neapolitain barber. He paid me twenty-five lire a week, and also allowed me to keep any tips I got—he had to do this, otherwise he'd have had to pay me thirty-five lire himself. So at last I'd found work. I was happy.

When my wife came out of hospital, we went to live with a cousin of mine in the Marinella. I used to go back and visit my foster mother quite often, though, and now that I was earning a bit I did what I could to help her. Her husband had been an outside railway porter, and those of his mates who were still working clubbed together and gave him a percentage of their takings. But this was hardly enough to live off, and he could certainly never afford to buy himself any little luxury like a cigar, or even a glass of wine. I knew how much he craved for them, so I was pleased when I had enough to be able to treat him to these small pleasures—after all, he'd done so much for me. I also liked being able to step in and make peace when they'd started to wrangle over some paltry sum she found he'd kept back for himself. Just imagine, having to go in for little subterfuges like that when you're over seventy! He could only buy himself one pipeful of tobacco a week: when he'd smoked that, he would carefully scrape out all the dottle and chew it, just to get a taste of the real thing. On Saturday nights, he used to come home a bit tight, and he'd rub his damp moustaches fondly against my cheek and sigh: 'Poor boy, poor boy . . .'

Then we had a row with my cousin, and decided to leave Rome: so we packed up and came back to Palermo.

I knew my father by sight because people had pointed him out to me, but I'd never exchanged a word with him. I had spoken to my grandfather, though: sometimes when I passed him in the street I used to beg a few nickels off him. Anyhow, when we found ourselves back in Palermo without a thing to call our own except a bit of household linen, and only a very little money which we'd managed to save up in Rome, I decided that I'd have to go and see my father. Of course as we were strangers to one another, I felt no natural affection for him—I couldn't even feel he *was* my father: but all the same, I had to go and see him—there was nothing else I could do. Well, he said we could come and live with him. He was married, and had several children. His wife didn't exactly welcome us with enthusiasm—but since he was boss in that house, and he'd invited us, she couldn't do much about it.

My father had fallen on very hard times. He'd been sacked from his job with the Council for being a Constitutional Socialist. When we first moved in, I became the provider: out of my savings, I had to buy food for the whole family. My father had become a *spicciafaccende* himself by this time—of course he had plenty of friends in the Town Hall.

There's one particular evening that stands out in my memory. I'd been out, and when I came home I found my stepsisters whining and grumbling because they were hungry and there was nothing to eat in the house. As I came in, one of them said to me: 'Papa's got some money, Gino, but he won't buy us any food.' 'We'll see about that,' I said, and off I went to find him. When I asked him if it was true that he had some money, he said yes, he had—but it didn't belong to him: a client had given it to him to get her some papers she needed. I was amazed at his honesty, knowing quite well what crooks most of the *spiccia-faccende* in Palermo are. They'll double-cross anyone, and most of them are in league with various officials on the Council or in the police or in the magistrates' courts—they have friends all over the place. If there's any false document you want, you can be quite sure of getting it through them.

We didn't stay long with my father. His wife had made up her mind to get rid of us, and shall I tell you what she did? At night, as we lay on our mattresses on the floor, she started chucking pebbles at us to make us believe the house was haunted. The first time, my wife was really scared. She'd got up in the night to go to the lavatory, but she came back shaking with fright, and said: 'Gino! There are ghosts in the house!'— the 'ghosts' had just flung a handful of pebbles at her. But soon we got our own back. In the room where my father and stepmother slept there was a little shrine, and on it stood a lighted candle, which we could also see from where we slept on the other side of the partition. So one night, as soon as the pebbles started coming over, I picked up a shoe and chucked it straight at the little altar so that the candle went out. 'The ghosts! The ghosts!' I shrieked—and then, wrapping myself in a sheet, I ran round to their side and jumped onto my dear stepmother's bed and gave her a good slapping about the face. Next morning, I kept a perfectly straight face when they all started talking about the ghosts, and when my stepmother told about what had happened in the night I burst out: 'What! So there *are* ghosts here? Well, we're not staying another night in a haunted house —we're off!'

So we moved out, and I rented a barber's shop.

You've no idea how careful a barber has to be not to give his customers the slightest cause for offence—for a mere trifle, they'll walk out on him and never come back. I've lost customers simply through not helping them into their over- coats or straightening their jackets exactly to their liking. The slightest little thing—if you leave so much as a single hair on a man's chin, or if you don't bow to him as low as the barber across the way, that's the last you'll see of him. You should have heard me when a new customer came in to open an account! 'What is your honoured name, Sir?' or: 'Would the gentleman be so kind as to give me his name?' I'd say obsequi- ously, with my pencil poised over the book. If you're a barber's assistant, you generally have to work very long hours. One barber I worked for in Rome did at least stick to a timetable, but the Neapolitain chap I told you about, being more of a Southerner, always refused to put up his shutters before his rival across the way had closed his—and as the barber opposite didn't want to be the first to shut up shop either, I usually didn't get home till about ten o'clock at night.

One day when we were still living in my father's house, I'd come across a photograph of a smartly dressed girl, and I asked my father who she was. 'That's your sister,' he said: 'your real sister—she's your mothers' daughter too. She's seven years older than you.' She was living with an uncle, he told me. Later, I found out her address, and decided to get in touch with her. I wrote her a letter. In order to get her to consent to see me at all, I had to pretend that I had a message for her from another uncle who lived in Rome. I wasn't allowed to go and see her at her own place, of course—even though the uncle whose house she was living in was my own uncle too. It's all this damned bourgeois respectability: people are so anxious to keep up appearances that they'll shirk their responsibilities, and hide their natural feelings, and even deny their own flesh and blood. If only my father had had the guts to say 'That's my son,' as soon as I was born, like my mother did, mine would have been a very different story . . .

But to go back: my sister agreed to meet me somewhere else —at a cousin's place. Well, I went along, and my cousin introduced us to each other, and then left us alone. We sat down on a settee, and for a few minutes there was complete silence. I felt terribly awkward—was I meant to speak first, or should I wait for her to say something? At last I plucked up courage and blurted out: 'Why d'you live with our uncle and not with Papa?' 'Because Uncle hasn't any children of his own,' she said. 'He's grown fond of me—he loves me like a father, and he's given me a good education. But tell me—where have you been all this time? Papa told me I had a brother, but I could never find out whree you'd got to.' I told her I hadn't known till quite recently that I even had a sister.

Then she began to ask me all sorts of questions: what school had I been to, was I a Catholic, was I a Fascist . . . (this was during the Fascist regime). I told her I'd only got as far as the Sixth Elementary class, and that I'd never really bothered my head about religion or politics. She was amazed that I wasn't a Catholic or a Fascist, and at once began to lecture me on these subjects. She'd got a degree in Literature herself, and she was really quite taken aback when I said that if I'd been lucky enough to have the sort of education she'd had, no doubt I'd have got a degree too, and become a Catholic and a Fascist into the bargain!

I simply couldn't manage to squeeze out a drop of brotherly affection for her. They talk of the call of the blood—but hers certainly didn't call to mine! Before I left, we agreed to see more of each other, but I felt I really didn't care whether we did or not.

However, we did meet again, one day in the street. She was on her way to the Fascist party headquarters in Piazza Bologni to renew her party card, and she asked me to accompany her there. But as we were walking along she warned me that if I should see a shortish young man coming towards us, I was to leave her at once, and pretend I was nothing to do with her. This was her fiancé, she said, and she was afraid he might be jealous—but of course what this really meant was that she didn't want anyone to know I was her brother.

Well, that was the end of it as far as I was concerned: I had no wish to see her again after that. We didn't meet again for a long time, not till after the war when we both came to our father's funeral. She was married by then, and for a while we were quite friendly, and I went to her house from time to time. Then one Christmas Day she invited me to supper there. I arrived in good time, but just as she was dishing up there was a ring at the door. 'Oh heavens!' she exclaimed, 'it must be some of my in-laws! Quick, Gino—hide: they mustn't see you!' I cleared out without a word, and never set foot in her place again.

In Palermo, the police informers, the narks, are the *cioccolattari*. The *cioccolattari* generally work in gangs of four or five, and practically all of them have police records. They run this kind of lottery which is a regular swindle. First, they buy about four hundred chocolates. They unwrap about one hundred of these, and stick in tiny slips of paper with numbers on, the lowest ten, the highest three thousand, or even four or five thousand. These chocolates are then wrapped up again and mixed with the three hundred or so unnumbered ones: but first, the foil round the ones with the high numbers, five hundred and upwards, is carefully marked with tiny dots so that the *cioccolattari* themselves can recognise them. Then they're ready to begin the raffle.

To attract a crowd, the *cioccolattari* start clowning about and playing the fool, hitting each other, doing conjuring tricks— producing an egg from a hat and all that sort of thing. If business is slow, the expert among them will take over and warm things up a bit. When the people begin to gather round, they stage fake contests among their confederates, and the 'winners' are allowed to have first dip at the chocolates. Of course by the time the crowd start buying theirs, the *cioccolattari* and their mates are pretty sure to have already fished out all the high numbers, so that the crowd get only the empty chocolates or, if they're lucky, the ones worth one or two hundred lire. If by any chance the *cioccolattari* should slip up and let one of the crowd get the five thousand lire chocolate, they can easily get round that. When the lucky winner holds up his slip to claim the prize, they get indignant and make out he's trying to cheat them —and to prove it, they produce the five thousand lire slip them- selves: a duplicate, of course, from the false bottom of the hat.

There must be about two hundred *cioccolattari* in Palermo. Obviously they wouldn't be allowed to run this lottery, which is nothing but an American style of swindle, if they weren't in league with the police: all lotteries and games of chance, even the straight ones, are illegal. The *cioccolattari* also do card tricks —'now you win and now you lose'—and various conjuring tricks, and so on.

Just about every quarter in Palermo has its *cioccolattari*. You get these retired criminals who were once the terror of the Capo and the Albergheria but who've now turned police informer. It's not really their fault, poor devils—instead of helping them to find some sort of decent work and make a new life for themselves, the authorities simply take advantage of their wretched state, and of their—what d'you call it?—their guilt complex about their past life, to push them under still further, and use them for their own ends. As long as they manage to remain 'men of honour', as they say, these old lags at least have a certain standing, even if it's only among the rest of the underworld: but once they've been forced to turn traitor, they lose all their old friends, everything—they're universally hated and despised.

The whole system here is based on patronage: it's this that governs the relationship between the authorities and the rest of us, between the poor devils who eat one day and starve the next and the gentry they depend on—the gentry who'll look after them so long as they toe the line. For instance, take the hawkers who sell tripe and lights: tripe and lights are hard to come by, and consequently they regard the merchant they get their supplies from as God Almighty. They know he only has to withdraw his favours—and they'll die of starvation. So his word is law as far as they're concerned, and of course the poor wretches will vote for whoever this pocket Caesar tells them: it's as much as their livelihood is worth to go against his will— and in any case they don't give a damn for politics themselves, usually. The petty despots who blackmail them this way are generally *mafiosi* acting on orders from higher up. And talking of the Mafia, let me tell you one of their favourite rackets. The shop of a tradesman who's already paid them his protection money is broken into and looted, and his 'protectors' assure him they'll comb the various quarters of the city and recover his goods for him. Well, in due course, the goods are found and restored to him—but at a price: he has to pay another substantial fee because, as they say, 'the boys must have their "bread".'

At the moment, I'm working as an itinerant barber—I haven't got a shop of my own any more. And of course I'm still an active member of my trade union, and of the Communist Party. I attend to my regular customers in their own homes, on certain fixed days. But the trouble is there aren't enough of them. However, lots of people know me well by sight, particularly in the Capo, and when they see me coming along with my bag the chaps bring out their chairs and a bowl of hot water, and I shave them there on their own doorsteps. That way, I just manage to scrape together enough for me and my family to live on.

But what makes my life such a fearful strain is that every morning as I set out I know that I've simply got to make so much that day. I go and call on one of my customers, and while I'm busy shaving him I'm already thinking of the fifty lire I'm going to get . . . only to be told when I've finished: 'I'll pay you tomorrow.' That happens so often. And if a customer falls ill, how can I ever get back the money he owes me? We've been married sixteen years now, and we still haven't been able to afford half the household stuff we need. Till recently, we've been living on the third floor of a tumbledown house in a room thirteen feet long by eight feet wide. Just imagine it—all eight of us crammed in there. But a few days ago the house started to really collapse, and it was declared dangerous, and we were moved out. They've put us up temporarily in this school, along with eighteen other families; the rest were sent to the Feliciuzza. But in five days time the school term starts again, so we'll have to shift—and what'll become of us then I just don't know.

Every month, I go and get my unemployment card renewed. For nine years my name's been down at the Labour Exchange, and I've never had the offer of so much as a single day's work. And what makes it even worse is the fact that owing to the leg injury I got in the war I'm officially registered as a Disabled Ex-Serviceman—and there's a law which makes it obligatory that all men who come into this category should be found employment.

I went along only yesterday to get my card stamped: exactly

the same old routine. I handed in my card to the official—poor devil, it's no wonder he's nearly out of his mind: the amount of work he has to cope with would be enough to keep five or six men busy. It's nearly driving him crazy—no wonder he flies off the handle at the least little thing, he's a mass of nerves. I'm really sorry for him.

It's funny, you know, I find nowadays I'm even sorry for the cops! When I was a kid, it was quite different—I couldn't stand the sight of them then: they regarded me as a menace, and hunted me and persecuted me, and I hated them in return. But in fact I see now that they weren't personally responsible—they just didn't realise what they were doing. I've gradually come to understand their position, and to sympathise with them—I've realised that they're not really to blame for the things they do: they're just one more class of workers exploited by the State. When I was little, just the sight of the police was enough to petrify me—I'd react like a rabbit caught in the headlights of a car. But now when I meet them I just feel sorry for them. In all these years, their mentality hasn't altered the slightest bit. They haven't taken a single step forward. Poor devils, they still haven't a clue.

Anyway, I was telling you about the scene at the Labour Exchange. The confusion there is frightful—everyone pushing and shoving, packed together, trampling on one another.

'Quiet please!' someone shouts, and the official begins to read off a list of names: 'Mazzola, Ganci, Di Maggio . . .'

'Present!'

'Present!'

'Di Maggio—where's Di Maggio?'

'He's not here.'

'Here, would you mind passing this up for me please.'

'Let's see—isn't that mine?'

'No!'

Meanwhile the crowd are all grumbling and cursing: 'It's a scandal—it's disgusting. Is this what they call keeping order?'

'There's only one way to clear up this place: chuck a bomb in!'

G

'Shut up—if they hear you talk like that they'll have you arrested, like that bloke the other day.'

There are women in the crowd too, all crushed in among the men. A young chap takes advantage of the confusion to feel up the girl next to him, with his other hand in his trouser pocket.

Then it starts to rain, and the crowd outside surges forward trying to get under cover: the crowd inside pushes back.

'Back! Back! Keep back!' shouts the cop on duty at the door. But they won't be kept out—they go on shoving and struggling, the whole crowd swaying backwards and forwards. A disabled man starts trying to elbow his way through.

'Your papers please!' shouts the cop. 'Where do you think you're going?'

'Minasola! Minasola!' someone yells, and the door slams shut. Then it opens again:

'Excuse me, have they called Geraci yet?'

'Please—can I have my card back?'

'Come again tomorrow.'

'But I'm ill . . .'

'Well, what do you expect *me* to do about it?'

It's not a Labour Exchange—it's a Tower of Babel!

Sometimes, I think to myself: 'Here I am, forty-two, and what have I got to show for all those years? Nothing . . .' But then I comfort myself with the thought that at least now I'm spending part of my life trying to help others so that they won't have to go through what I did. And besides, I realise I must carry on because I have a responsibility towards my family, towards my children. And also towards the Party—because I am certain it was my experience with the Party, the way it backed me up in my struggles, that made a new man of me. Often in the morning when I get up early to go out to work, I stop beside the little bed where my two youngest children sleep, and I bend down and give the baby a kiss. At least I'm giving them the love and security I never had. 'Even a chap like me isn't completely useless,' I tell myself. But all the same . . .

The wretched life I had when I was young has left a permanent scar on my character—I'm still unsure of myself: it's given me a sort of inferiority complex, which I've never managed to get rid of. Although I've learnt to look at life very differently, and though I'm really almost a different person now, this feeling of inferiority still dogs me. And of course it comes over me always at the worst times: in my political activities, for instance, when I'm trying to stand up for some democratic principle— just when I'm most in need of strength of character, it undermines me.

If I had to keep on like this for the rest of my life, fighting and fighting, constantly pitting my strength against my surroundings and against other people, I'm sure I'd lose heart. But there's one thought that keeps me going: if you have oil and vinegar together in a bottle, and you keep shaking it, they're completely blended so that you can't tell them apart. But as soon as you stop shaking, the oil will start coming to the top. To me, the oil stands for the truth—and the truth, by the very nature of things, can't be kept down for ever: like the oil, sooner or later it's bound to come to the surface.

It's because I'm so certain of this that, while I'm struggling to support my family, I'm still able to continue fighting side by side with the Comrades for the good of the community. Whenever the need arises for people to rally to the defence of a particular family or a particulr neighbourhood, I'm always ready to be called on, always ready to take up the cause. Here, read this letter I've just received from a Comrade:

'I am writing to thank you and all the other Comrades for your kindness to me during the months when I was doing my military service in Palermo. I can't tell you how much it meant to me. Thank you for helping me to understand so much more about politics—I'll put my new knowledge to good use, I promise you. Thank you, too, for the unforgettable dinner you gave me on my last evening there— and thank you for all your hospitality and friendliness towards me and my other army comrades. I'll always remember you, and when I'm an old man and take my grandchildren on my knees, instead of telling them fairy stories, I'll tell them about the good Comrades in Palermo who fought so bravely to make a better, more progressive Sicily—a Sicily freed from the exploiters and oppressors who were sucking away her life blood. And of course I'll tell them, too, about the brotherly hand you held out to me and the other Comrades who came to Palermo from far away Emilia . . .'

# Ignazio, the junk man

NONE of the men in the Cortile Cascino—Via D'Ossuna, Cortile Grotta—have ever worked in the builders' yards. Practically all of us are junk men and rag pickers—we've never been able to get any other kind of work. The women earn a bit by doing washing. Just occasionally one of the young men may be taken on somewhere for a short spell as a builders' labourer, but that sort of job never lasts—it's too uncertain. They always come back to the rag and bone trade. At least there's this to be said for it: it is a more or less permanent job.

About seven years ago, there was an outbreak of typhus here, and about ten people died of it. They sent the *carabinieri* along: we weren't allowed to leave the block for fear of spreading the infection—no one was allowed out at all.

This place stinks—the whole courtyard's one mass of mud and filthy puddles. In the morning most of the women go and empty the slops onto the railway line over there, but there are some sluts who don't bother, they just fling everything out into the courtyard, and the muck piles up around that open drain where the stagnant water gathers. In winter, the place gets so deep in slush and filth that we have to have the firemen in. They pump off a little water, and syphon some up from the cellars, and then leave it at that. 'That's the best we can do,' they say, and off they go. There's been more than one outbreak of typhus here—it's the lice that spread the infection, you know. Another time, two people died, and dozens of kids went down with it. It's generally the kids who die of typhus.

That time I was telling you about, when they stationed the *carabinieri* here to see that we kept within bounds, our food was cooked for us and brought round to the Cortile in huge cauldrons. The *carabinieri* used to come along first and blow a blast on a bugle to announce that the food was ready, and hundreds of us would hurry out with our saucepans and pots and empty cans and so on, and queue up in a long line, like soldiers. It wasn't charity—they had to feed us because we weren't allowed out, and so we couldn't go to work or anything. When we wanted to relieve ourselves, we just had to do it in the courtyard. Sometimes, though, we might get decent *carabinieri* who'd let us men go out to our usual place on the railway lines. But it was terrible, because they put some sort of medicine in the food they gave us, to kill the germs—and it must have been a purge, because every one of us, men, women and children, all fifteen hundred of us, had diarrhoea.

It's no wonder we get typhus here—look at the filth, look at the way the houses are all crowded together. There's no water laid on, and we live eight or ten or even twelve to a room. You can't even call them rooms, mostly: little cells. Most of them just have beaten earth floors, and some of them are nothing more than dark windowless caves. Lots of families don't have any furniture at all—not even chairs: they sit on stones, or on empty tins. As for lice, there are bushels of them. In that typhus epidemic, when they laid out the dead they had so many lice all over their bodies it was really horrible. The sanitary squads came round and scattered insecticide powder everywhere to try and get rid of the lice—inside the houses, all over the streets, everywhere. They even dusted it over us—men and women alike, we went and unfastened our clothes so that they could sprinkle it down inside.

This winter, the rain was so heavy that some of the houses flooded. The inspectors came along, and had a look round, and went off again. The families whose rooms were under water piled up their mattresses and pillows and various other odds and ends on handcarts, and went trundling round the streets trying to find other rooms. There were dozens of other homeless families, too, from other quarters that had also been flooded out, and in the end the Council had to take action. The whole lot were rounded up and taken to the empty sheds in the market. The men were put at one end, and the women at the other—hundreds of them, all herded in there together like horses packed in stalls. They had to sleep on the ground, with only their few miserable blankets to cover them. After they'd been there four or five days, they protested, and demanded to be rehoused. But all that happened was that each family was given fifteen hundred or two thousand lire and sent back where they came from—they were told there just wasn't anywhere else for them to go.

Every morning, we men go out and relieve ourselves on the railway lines. It's been the custom as long as I can remember— they used to do it in my father's day, too. Sometimes they catch us at it, though, and we're fined 2,500 lire for committing a nuisance. Fancy having to pay for that—and such a hell of a price, too! The women do it indoors, and the kids usually just squat down in the street, or else they do it on the railway line too. Six months ago, a five year old boy from one of those houses just down there was squatting on the line when a train came along and killed him. And another time a kid who'd gone to sleep in the tunnel was run over and killed.

And to think that all this goes on just a couple of hundred yards from the Cathedral, in the heart of Palermo!

As I said before, most of the men here work as junk men and rag-pickers, and the women as washerwomen. There are some people who haven't got any work at all, and others who earn a few lire by making little flags with pictures of Saint Rosalia on them. Quite a few of the women here earn their living on the streets—their beats are in other parts of Palermo, though: here, the houses are so much on top of each other that the neighbours would soon spot what they were up to, and of course they don't want anyone to know what they're doing.

Hardly any of the kids ever go to school—they play about all day long in the filthy courtyard. As soon as the little girls are twelve or thirteen, they start looking around for husbands. They practically always marry someone from their own courtyard—the little washerwoman marry the little rag-pickers!

I'd been a prisoner in the war, and I came back to Palermo in the October of 1944—I arrived on the 8th of October, after a journey lasting a whole month. When I got home, I found my family half dead with hunger—I mean my parents, of course: at

that time I wasn't even married myself. Next morning, a couple
of friends of mine came round. They asked if I'd got a job, and
I said no, so they asked me if I'd go and help them move a pile
of wood they'd found on a bomb site. Well, I went along with
them: but just as we were collecting the wood together, a lady
came up and asked what I was doing there, because it was her
house that had been bombed. Then she called the *carabinieri*,
and accused us of having stolen her furniture and stuff from
among the ruins. The *carabinieri* went round and searched my
place, and of course they didn't find anything, but I was taken
along to the police station and interrogated by the Sergeant.
When he asked to see my papers, of course I couldn't produce
any: I'd only arrived home the day before, and I hadn't yet got
any papers. So they put me in prison—me, who'd never in my
life been in any sort of trouble with the police. I was in there for
about five months before my trial came up; then I was taken
to court and charged with attempted theft, and sentenced to
twelve months.

Of course I had no one to defend me—how could I pay for a
lawyer to defend me when I hadn't even the money for a bite to
eat, and my family were starving? I appealed against my
sentence, though, and got it reduced to six months. But still,
I'd blotted my copy-book: I've done a stretch, and now according to the law I'm a criminal.

That was the first and the last time I was in prison—thank
goodness, I've managed to keep clear of the police ever since.
But I've had a hard life all the same—believe me, I've been
through a lot. In the junk business it's impossible to make
enough to keep your family, and so my wife has to go out to
work too, as a cleaner.

Once I was ill for eighteen months on end with the Maltese
Fever. I can't read or write—you won't find many around here
who can. I get up at seven in the morning, summer and winter
alike, and trudge round the streets with my handcart shouting:
'Any old rags, old iron or lumber?' I buy up all sorts of old
junk and rags, as well as old iron. You don't get much for old
iron: thirteen lire the kilo. It's hardly worth selling at the price.

I work for a chap who gives me the cash to buy with; the handcart belongs to him too—I hire it for fifty lire a day. Some days, I may make three hundred lire, but there are whole weeks when I earn nothing at all. Of course you may just strike it lucky and make a thousand lire in one go, or even more—but I don't need to tell you that hardly ever happens. At mid-day, we have to pack it in—no one sells any more after twelve o'clock, so that's the end of our hopes for the day. Just about all the men on this courtyard are in the same trade—there must be about two hundred of us junk men around here. All the old iron and copper and rags in Palermo find their way into this quarter.

Another thing we buy is orange and mandarine and lemon peel, at ten lire a kilo; then we sell it to the wholesalers who supply the factories where they make orange and lemon essence. The wholesalers charge sixteen to eighteen lire for a kilo of peel. A lot of the kids in this quarter go round the streets collecting fag ends, then they peel off the paper and sell the tobacco that's left. They don't spend the money on themselves, though: they give the few lire they get to their families—it all helps out. Some of the poor devils who work in the builders' yards can't afford to smoke real cigarettes, so they buy ten or twenty lire's worth of these shreds of tobacco and roll their own fags. The kids go into the centre of Palermo—Via Libertà, around the Massimo Theatre, all the most crowded places—to collect the fag ends. If the police catch them at it, though, they're taken off to the Malaspina borstal. It's against the law to collect cigarette ends. It's a shocking offence, apparently: a real disgrace. I'll say it's a disgrace—to the authorities themselves, and well they know it!

In wet weather, there's nothing doing for us junk men. During the winter we can't go out to work often—we only put in a few odd days. We buy our bread and our *pasta* on tick, but as no shopkeeper will give credit for more than a thousand to fifteen hundred lire at a time, we have to go round running up debts at all the shops in the neighbourhood.

As I said, business is over for us by about mid-day, but in the afternoon you'll find quite a lot of us still hanging about in the road by the level crossing. That's the way to most of the wholesalers' warehouses and junk depots, and there's always a hope of picking up an extra lira or two if someone should come along with a bit of old iron to sell, or a few rags or something. To pass the time, we play cards, or else go to the *cantina*. The chaps who haven't any money just stand around in the sun. In the *cantina*, we talk about the prices of old iron and copper, and what sort of a morning we've had, and how much we've made, and we do our best to cheer each other up.

'Well, how much did you get today?' I'll ask one of the chaps.

'Five hundred lire,' he may say, or: 'Not a thing.'

'Hard luck!' we say, and do what we can to raise his spirits.

I give you my word everything I've been telling you is absolutely true: I know this life inside out—my family have been in the junk trade in this quarter for a hundred and ten years.

When a chap goes home with his pockets empty, as likely as not there'll be a row: 'What have you been doing in the streets all morning!' his wife shouts: 'Didn't anyone call you?'

'I can't help it—it's not my fault if nobody calls me, it's just bad luck,' says the man, hoping to goodness he'll be able to make a bit the next day. If he doesn't, there'll be a flaming row, and it'll end up with them coming to blows.

Our quarter's what you might call a dead end: we never get to know anything outside the junk trade. We're not interested in anything that happens in the rest of Palermo—unless it's a murder.

Nobody's the least religious around here. At election times, though, the priest comes round with one or two gents and they hand out *pasta* to try and get us to vote for them. The ones that come round most are the Monarchists; they have little cards printed with addresses of where we can go to get a kilo of free *pasta*. Most people vote as they're told to vote: they're scared stiff at the thought of what would happen to them if it came out that they hadn't voted for the right party. Hardly any of us go to church—there's no such thing as Sundays or Feast days for the likes of us. On Sundays all we think about is where on earth we're going to find some food to put on the table.

This is a tough quarter. Once, two strangers came along and started taking photographs, and one of the blokes who lives here—he was rolling drunk, even though it was only half past ten in the morning—he was furious, and before they could realise what was happening he'd reached out and grabbed the camera off them. People here don't like it when outsiders come and take pictures. Those two poor devils were terrified—it was touch and go whether or not he'd smash up their camera which was worth eighty thousand lire!

# Old Andrea, the spicciafaccende

HERE in Palermo, the *affarista* (or *spicciafaccende* as he is commonly known), in executing his legitimate business, is subjected on the one hand to the calumnies of the common people who are his clients and, on the other hand, to the mistrust and suspicion of the authorities.

Originally, *affarismo* might be said to have been a perfectly respectable profession: recently, however, it has fallen into considerable disrepute, due to the large numbers of unemployed persons to be found in this occupation at the present time. There are said to be approximately one thousand *spicciafaccende* here in Palermo, but in my opinion five hundred would be a more accurate estimate.

These unemployed persons, finding themselves constrained and obliged by dire necessity, take it upon themselves to stand about all day in the vicinity of the various administrative offices, in the hope of obtaining commissions from such members of the public as require assistance in obtaining and filling in various official documents. In exchange for an extremely modest remuneration, they may have to spend as much as a whole day at the offices of the civil courts, or at the Tribunal, or at the Registrar's office, or at the Magistrates' courts, as the case may be, in order to obtain, from the appropriate office, either marriage or birth or death certificates, licenses, contracts, legal documents, penal certificates, papers relative to pending court cases, and various other official documents of a similar nature.

Serving his client in this manner, the unfortunate *affarista* (who is no doubt disliked by the same) nevertheless earns, by way of remuneration for all this conscientious, distasteful and fatiguing work, no more than a tiny little sum scarcely sufficient to procure him a morsel of hard bread. Now, what is the reason for this? Let us take a hypothetical case as an example: let us take your client who is desirous to obtain a birth certificate. The document itself costs 55 lire. Let us suppose the *affarista* charges one hundred lire: what does he make? A mere forty-five lire. Yet for this trifling sum he has first to obtain and fill in the application for the document, then return to the office the following day in order to collect the said document, and finally he has to consign it into the hands of his client. That is just one example.

The law against *zuinismo*—which is to say, against bribery and corruption—was not intended to penalise the unfortunate *affarista*, but nevertheless, the heads of the various offices, having undue regard to this law, issue positive instructions to the effect that no *affarista* shall present himself in person at the counters: and thus begins our *Via Crucis* in the struggle against starvation. For it follows that when the individual who is endeavouring to carry on business as an *affarista* wishes to oblige his clientèle, he can only acquire the necessary documents through the favour of some clerk or person employed in the office concerned, in exchange for a far from negligible consideration. Furthermore, since the negotiations with the said clerk relative to the documents in question cannot be conducted on the premises of the offices concerned, the *affarista* is obliged to entertain the clerk at his own expense, either in a cafe, or, indeed, in his own home.

As I was saying, the *affarista* is generally unpopular among his clients, being considered by them to be excessively lucrative. And this is solely because the persons who avail themselves of his services believe him to be somewhat too avaricious and venal in the negotiations relative to his fee. Be that as it may, I nevertheless maintain that it is only logical and natural— indeed, to use the proper term, only *human*—that the individual who finds himself, due to unemployment, constrained by sheer necessity to undertake the business of *affarista*—(and this, may I add, not for the sake of personal gain but solely in order that he may provide a morsel of bread for his spouse and for his offspring, his own flesh and blood)—it being, as I say, pro- hibited to present himself at the counters (as is the right of any ordinary citizen), and finding himself obliged, therefore, to have recourse to the employees of the office concerned, in exchange for a remuneration exceeding what he himself is supposed to earn . . . But let us return to our previous example: given that the birth certificates costs fifty-five lire, and add to that the fifty lire one is obliged to give the clerk, it is clearly insufficient to charge your client a hundred lire. In order that I myself may have a hundred and fifty lire, it stands to reason that I am obliged to charge my client two hundred.

The life of the *affarista* is indeed a difficult and exhaustive one. In the first place, he has to find the clientèle from whom he is to obtain the commission to deal with the matter or matters in hand; then he has to contact the clerk in the appropriate office, and in all likelihood he will have to return several times to wait for the clerk in the vicinity of the offices at closing time, before he receives the requisite documents; and finally he has to consign the said documents into the hands of his client. Furthermore, since the domicile of the same is frequently situated outside Palermo, this will necessitate him to deduct from his already exceedingly modest profit the additional expense of the tram fare. That is what the life of the *affarista* consists in.

The public find it necessary to employ the *affarista* for a wide variety of reasons: either in order to avoid having to queue up for hours amongst the rest of the crowd; or on account of the lengthy bureaucratic complications involved; or because the opening hours of the Government offices are too restricted (in theory they are intended to open at nine and close at one, but in practice they do not open until nine thirty, and then close again at twelve thirty); or else, due to illiteracy, members of the public find themselves obliged to have recourse to the services of your *spicciafaccende,* who will be able to obtain a more prompt settlement of the matter in hand by means of negotiations with certain employees in the offices concerned. Some twenty per cent of the population of Palermo, being illiterate and yet unable to afford the full services of the *spicciafaccende,* will nevertheless employ him in the initial stages of the transaction—namely, to fill in on their behalf the official application form for the document required, for which he will receive a fee of approximately ten to twenty lire. A further forty per cent of the population of Palermo are pleased to be able to avail themselves of the services of the *spicciafaccende* for the more prompt despatch of their business without the necessity of themselves having to lose one or more days' work. In addition, some ten per cent of the local notabilities employ us because they do not wish to demean themselves by wasting their valuable time on anything so tedious and common as the lengthy bureaucratic processes involved.

You may observe large numbers of *affaristi* in the vicinity of the Law Courts, waiting to obtain commissions relative to legal documents; and similarly in the vicinity of the Municipal offices. Many of the ushers and doorkeepers also act as *spicciafaccende* on their own account.

Even under the Fascist regime, *zuinismo* (by which is meant bribery and corruption) was illegal: but not *affarismo*. *Zuinismo* concerns your party who is paid to go round advising and persuading the clients of various lawyers, or doctors, or hotels, or shops, to withdraw their custom and transfer their patronage elsewhere, to such and such another establishment. But *affarismo* was never an offence, as was clearly vindicated by a court case in 1936. (Or perhaps it was 1937.) A certain retired fireman by name of Caciotto, being at that date in receipt of a small pension, was apprehended by the judicial authorities and charged with *affarismo*. He was brought before the Fifth Penal Section of the Tribunal of Palermo, the presiding Justice being the late Judge Fazio, (subsequently deceased), and Counsel for the Defence being Signor Giovanni Rosano, (as at this day still living). Now, in Caciotto's defence, it was argued that the letter of the law should in this case be disregarded, since it had clearly been the intention of the legislative body, according to the spirit of the law, to make a distinction between the crime of *zuinismo* and the legitimate pursuit of *affarismo*. Caciotto was accordingly acquitted, on the grounds that *affarismo* does not *per se* constitute an offence. And yet they'll still arrest my colleagues and I just for giving tips!

Unless and until action is taken for the social reclamation of men, no progress of mankind can ever take place, and neither will humanity ever acquire the necessary habit of mutual assistance and co-operation throughout every sphere of life.

In the majority of cases, the *spicciafaccende* themselves are none too well educated: but nevertheless they do tend to be a more intelligent type of person, with greater intellectual capacities. Besides, we learn a considerable amount from our continual contact with the educated employees at the various offices; and if ever we find that something is beyond our powers, the official concerned will always elucidate the matter for us.

Since my livelihood depends on what I can earn as a *spicciafaccende,* I have to exercise great caution in order not to offend my clients: if you are a Monarchist, I am a Monarchist likewise; if you're a Fascist, then I'm a Fascist too; if you're Christian Democrat, so am I. If I should displease my client in any way whatsoever, I may lose five hundred lire. I carry copies of all the party membership cards in my pocket—I'm affiliated to them all!

I trust I have given you a brief, clear, and accurate account of the life of the *affarista.*

*Affarismo* is not a profession: it is an occupation into which people are driven by unemployment.

# A group of schoolchildren[1]

*Cielo*    At school when we're given a problem, I try to help my friend and explain the problem to him, but the teacher won't let me.

*Libera*    Our teacher won't let us help each other, either. She says: 'You must work it out by yourselves.' If my friend doesn't understand it, I try and explain it to her—I don't just get her to copy it, I try and explain. But the teacher won't let us.

*Cielo*    Our teacher won't let us do any of our exercises together—he says if we do we'll only copy. Suppose you're given a problem, and you think and think about it—well, you'll probably find the answer. Then if you're friendly with the others you'll want to help them find the answer too—but our teacher hardly ever lets us help each other at all.

*Chiara*    I always copy my teacher, and I sing with her when she sings, and I copy my teacher when we're doing gym.

*Cielo*    Me and my friends at school chat during break. On Mondays, for instance, we tell each other about the film, say, or whatever else we've seen or done on Sunday. It's only during break, when we're having our snack, that we can get together with our friends and talk.

*Libera*    When our teacher goes out of the room—when she goes to talk to another teacher, for instance—then we can talk to our friends, and get to know each other better. But when the teacher's there, we all have to sit still and keep ourselves to ourselves. We can only get together and do things together when the teacher's

[1] For the children's ages, see page 11.

|          | not there, or else during break when she's just sitting there doing her knitting or reading the paper. |
| -------- | --- |
| *Amico* | I've got a friend I'd like to work out sums with—we always want to help each other—and our teacher does sometimes let us, but usually not. And it's just the same in our class as you others say—we can only get together with our friends when the teacher goes out. |
| *Ruggero* | Sometimes he pretends to go out of the classroom, but really he's hiding just outside the door. Then if we start to make a row he suddenly bursts into the room again, and he gets us all lined up against the wall, and makes us hold out our hands like this, and then he gets his great big stick and comes along the line hitting us all. |
| *Cielo* | The boys on the back benches say it doesn't hurt them so much. They're the poorest boys, you see, and they go out to work in the fields—breaking up wood, and loading it on carts, and hoeing, and so on—and so the skin of their hands gets all thick and tough. |
| *Amico* | Yesterday just before we broke up for the holidays, our teacher gave Toia two strokes of the cane on his legs, and said: 'Happy Easter!' The other boys didn't know whether to be frightened or laugh! |
| *Chiara* | When my teacher tells me to be quiet, I sit perfectly still, as if I was asleep, and so she gives me good marks. |
| *Danilo* | But do they teach any of you how to work together at all? Or how to play together, or how to set about finding things out together? |
| *Libera* | No, our school doesn't teach us how to get on with each other, or do anything together, or co-operate in any way. We get together at recreation time, but our teacher doesn't ever tell us what we ought to do to get on better with each other, or how each of us is supposed to organise herself so that it's possible to co-operate with the rest. |
| *Cielo* | They do *talk* about 'getting together', though, at school. When the priest comes, he preaches to us about |

what Jesus said—that we should all be brothers, that we should stick together, and love one another like brothers, and so on. But it's just words: they never try to teach us how we might get on better together.

Libera  Yes, it's just like Cielo says. And the priest also tells us that anyone who isn't a Catholic is damned!

Cielo  And he says that the Lord is our Master, and that we must serve him, because we are the servants of God.

Amico  The teacher's idea of what we should be like is just the same as the priest's—he'd like us to be just a sort of well drilled squad ready to carry out whatever order he cares to give us.

Chiara  When my teacher says: 'Right, start your work now!' —when she says that, I do my copying in my copy-book. I'm good at copying.

Bruna  Really I think it's true to say our school doesn't teach us to co-operate at all. What they want, rather, is for everyone to do their own work, and for everyone to think exactly the same—for instance, everyone ought to be Catholic. And everyone must do as the teacher says. You're not supposed to have your own opinion. Most of the teachers seem to want simply to drill us into neat, obedient squads.

It's only in the breaks that we really get together and make friends. We're not just sitting at a desk listening —we can discuss things then, and express our own opinions.

But in fact even us girls don't agree much among ourselves, because you get some from Catholic families, while others are liberals, or communists; and everyone prefers to make friends with other girls who share the same point of view. The class is really split up into a whole lot of little groups. And basically, of course, everybody's really only interested in their own things. We get this feeling of being united only in relation to the teacher—I mean, we're only a group in so far as we're opposed to the teacher. Out of about eight teachers, I can only think of two who would ever let us sit and work beside a friend—but none of them have ever taught us how to co-operate.

*Danilo*    Would you say that there's any sort of co-operation between you and your teachers?

*Cielo*    No, I'd say there was none.

*Bruna*    Our teacher might perhaps co-operate occasionally with whoever was top of the class. She'd say: 'Here, help me with this . . .' but you can't really call that co-operation—the teacher's just getting whoever's best in the class to help her.

*Cielo*    Or our teacher might leave a boy in charge of the class: 'I've got to go out,' he says: 'you must write up on the blackboard the name of anyone who talks, or anyone who misbehaves.'

*Chiara*    *We* do things together with *our* teacher. She says to us: 'You tell me the numbers and I'll write them up on the board.' Or else the teacher says: 'Throw that bit of paper in the waste paper basket,' and me and my friends all rush to throw it in the waste paper basket for her.

*Bruna*    I'll tell you what it's like really: we mustn't do anything to harm one another, we must respect our elders and betters, and so on—but we can't have opinions. There's no question of me first having my say, and then you having your say, and then discussing the thing till we reach some conclusion that suits us all. We mustn't do anything to *harm* one another—but there's no question of me actually *helping* you, or you helping me.

It's just the same sort of thing with school games. The kind of games the teachers make us play are usually just boring drill—it's only amongst ourselves that we ever play games in groups. For instance, one of the schoolteachers' favourites is the silence game: the whole class sits as still as possible, and the teacher calls up whoever is sitting stillest and quietest, and he goes and stands by the blackboard and looks carefully round the class at the rest of them and sees who's quietest, and writes his name on the board; and then *he* comes up to the board, and the first one goes and sits in the second one's place—and so on. But this so-called game isn't a game at all—it's just a trick to keep us all quiet when the teacher wants to read the paper. They play this game in all the elementary classes here —and the daft thing is, most of the kids like it!

*Amico*    Well, I like it too. At least it means that instead of being stuck in my own seat all the time I might get the chance to go and sit in someone else's, if I'm called up.

*Chiara*    And I like it too—it's nice to have a little walk.

*Bruna*    Yes, even I used to like it—because it was about the only game they ever let us play.

*Cielo and Libera*    But those sort of games are stupid.

(A few days later.)

*Danilo*    Well, I wonder if you've been having any more ideas about what we were discussing the other day. What would you say a group consisted of?

*Cielo*    A group is a collection of boys or girls or school friends who help each other, because they like each other, and so they form a group.

*Chiara*    A group is when you get into fours, or twos, or when you all line up together.

*Bruna*    What Chiara means is that in a group there should be some sort of order—but of course there's no need to be in twos or fours particularly. Cielo was saying that for it to be a proper group you must be in agreement: but it's more than just a matter of having some sort of order and saying: 'We all like each other.' You must also have some purpose—I mean some sort of good aim—otherwise you're not going to get anywhere.

*Libera*    In a group, there has to be one person who says: 'Let's all do such and such,' and then they all have a meeting to decide how the work should be shared out among them. That way, they get the thing done quicker, and better.

*Bruna*  Yes, I agree that the group should have a leader—but this leader mustn't just be someone who gives orders: his job should be to co-ordinate all the suggestions made by the rest of the group, and co-operate with them in planning and organising things properly.

*Amico*  You can't have a group if everyone is acting independently.

*Danilo*  Would you say the potatoes in a sack are a group?

*Chiara*  Yes.

*Libera*  They're a sack of potatoes!

*Amico*  They can't be a group, because they're not really alive.

*Libera*  No, they're just a collection of potatoes, they're not a group.

*Bruna*  Well, you can have a collection of children, or men, who aren't a group any more than a sack of potatoes is a group. It's not just being together that counts.

*Danilo*  Have any of you ever had any experience of being in charge of a group?

*Amico*  Yes, I have.

*Cielo*  So've I. But I suppose really that was more like a team. But sometimes I have taken charge, too, when we've got into a group of our own accord.

*Amico*  I've been left responsible sometimes, when the teacher went away.

*Libera*  In a team, you see, you have a captain, and the rest have to do whatever he says. But in a group it's different: instead of just obeying, or copying like so many parrots, each person has his own little job to do, his own particular contribution towards whatever it is that the group is working on.

*Ruggero*  I've never been in charge—but how d'you mean exactly, being in charge . . . being responsible . . . I don't quite see.

*Amico*  Well, being responsible means more or less the same as being in command.

*Bruna*     No—it isn't the same as being in command. Being responsible means knowing what you're doing, really understanding what's going on.

*Libera*    For instance, suppose the mistress in a nursery school isn't looking after the children properly and one of them gets hurt—well, she's in charge, and she's responsible.

*Danilo*    Do you like having responsibility? D'you like taking charge in a group?

*Amico*     Yes.

*Chiara*    Yes.

*Libera*    It's nice being in charge when you're good at something.

*Bruna*     I like being in a group, and I like being responsible, I don't know why.

*Ruggero*   Yes—for instance, if there's someone quarrelling and I stop them quarrelling.

*Bruna*     But a person shouldn't want to take charge just so as to get the admiration and respect of the others.

*Cielo*     The important thing is to have a sense of responsibility towards yourself and towards other people.
            The more responsibility you're allowed, the more ideas you'll have, and the better you'll get.

*Ruggero*   Yes, that's just what I was trying to say.

*Danilo*    Which do you like best: being with people older than yourselves, or the same age, or younger?

*Cielo*     I think I prefer playing with younger boys, or else ones of my own age.

*Amico*     I like being with younger ones.

*Ruggero*   Yes, I agee—I think they're better to play with.

*Chiara*    I like playing with children smaller than me, too.

*Libera*    Yes, I like playing with really little children, under five—I can pick them up and carry them. But I like girls of my own age as well, because we can talk and play together. And I like bigger ones, too—as long as they're nice!

*Bruna*     I think it depends entirely on whether they're nice or not: it doesn't matter at all whether they're younger or older than me, as long as I like them.

*Libera*   When I play with little children I feel just like a mother!

*Ruggero*   It's better playing with people younger than yourself.

*Amico*   Yes: when you play with younger boys, you don't quarrel with them—they don't quarrel because they're too young. But if you play with the older ones, you always quarrel.

*Cielo*   Yes, and it's difficult when you play with older boys because they try and boss you around—they want the game to go their way. The big boys aren't very easy to get on with. But when I play with smaller boys, it's *me* who says how we'll play!

*Libera*   I like telling the little children stories. They're sweet, they sit there listening with their eyes wide open . . .

*Danilo*   What sort of grown-ups do you like best?

*Cielo*   The ones we're most friendly with.

*Ruggero*   I like my Papa best!

*Bruna*   The ones who take us seriously—the ones who bother to talk to us, and discuss things with us. Not the sort of grown-up who just says: 'Yes yes, of course,' without even hearing what you've said, or who won't listen to you, or who just says 'no' without giving you any reason. We like the ones who understand.

*Amico*   I like grown-ups who are amusing, and tell funny jokes and stories, and make us laugh all the time.

*Cielo*   I like grown-ups who give us nice things; and I like the ones I know really well, and also the ones who like me.

*Bruna*   And I like being with grown-ups who I can learn things from.

*Danilo*   One more question: do you think this discussion we've been having here should be reported and written down for other people to read?

*Cielo*   No, I don't think so really, because if my teacher hears of it I'll get into trouble.

*Ruggero*   Well I think it should—I think it would be nice if other people could hear our arguments.

*Bruna*   Yes, I think so too. If our teachers read it, perhaps they'll wake up a bit and try to improve! And after all, in discussing things together like this we're only trying to be more responsible.

*Libera*   I think what we've been saying should be made public, because we've been giving our own opinions quite sincerely, and everything we've said is true, and also I think most of it's interesting.

*Cielo*   Yes, on second thoughts, I agree too. It should be reported. Everyone else agrees, and I think they're right, so I've changed my mind.

*Libera*   Another time, maybe one of us could be chairman of the meeting. When can we have another little meeting? Tomorrow, perhaps?

# *Sariddu: against war*

WHEN my call-up papers arrived, I had to give up my job. We had to report to military headquarters in Palermo, and when we arrived there, we were made to line up for the medical inspection. They told us we were going to Avellino. Before we left, they handed out our first issue of rations, and seven cigarettes and seven matches each. Then we went to the station, and at half past ten in the evening the train left. I'd never done a journey that long in my life before, and travelling all through the night like that made me feel as if we were going to the end of the world.

In the morning, we got out at Messina. There our escort left us, and we were on our own.

From Reggio to Salerno, we had to travel in goods vans. The train was rattling along at a terrific speed, and these cattle trucks were jerking and swaying about so much we were afraid they were about to fall to pieces, the train was going so fast. We got out at Salerno, and changed trains—but then we found we'd got on the wrong train, all thirty of us. (There were thirty of us going to Avellino.) We'd all just been following the squad leader. There wasn't another train for four hours, and so by the time we reached Avellino they'd given up expecting us. There was just this sergeant waiting there, and the minute he saw us he started bellowing like a bull: 'Where the hell have you been, you lousy bastards!' One of the blokes from Palermo told him he'd better keep a civil tongue in his head because we weren't soldiers yet—but he yelled out: 'You are soldiers already—fall in over there!' And we were marched off to the barracks. This was at one o'clock in the morning.

At six o'clock, reveille sounded. But of course, as we'd only just arrived, we reckoned that it didn't concern us, and so we pretended not to hear. But before long a corporal came in and began to shout at us. We staggered out of bed feeling like dead dogs, and then we were marched along to a great big room full of officers. We were called up in front of them one at a time, and after the first three or four had been stood there as markers, the rest were all lined up beside them, according to where they were allotted: 'You—Number 7 Company, such and such a platoon!' and so on. Then we were taken to a barrack-room and issued with bed, blankets, and so forth. Next, we had our hair cut: we all wore our hair long and wavy then, but they shaved it all off so we looked as if we had ringworm! Next morning: reveille, coffee—and then they announced we were going to start training.

We were all formed up by companies: for drill, they told us. Along came the corporal. We were drawn up three deep, and he called out: 'Attention! Company, quick march!'—and we were just like a flock of sheep, everyone out of step and out of line. 'Company, halt!' shouted the corporal, and it was a shambles—two hundred men all tumbling over each other because some of them stopped and the others ran into them from behind.

'Come on, come on,' said the corporal: 'we can't have bungling idiots like this around here. But we'll get you into shape by and by, just you wait!'

He called out the first three men, and drew a line on the ground, and lined them up on it. Then he called them to attention one by one. He went through the same business with each of us in turn. 'Atten . . . *shun*!' and he explained how we must stand: 'Head straight, chin up, chest out, body upright and stiff as a ramrod. Hands straight and to the sides, heels together and toes well out.' When he called us to attention, we had to give a little jump and bring our heels together with a click, all in one movement.

Then he made us stand at ease. We had to stamp one foot down firmly on the ground—'I want to *hear* that foot!' he kept shouting, making us stamp even harder. Those were the regulations, he said. You know the sentries in Palermo—well, they have a plank to stand on, just so that it'll make more noise when they stamp their foot down: it's supposed to be more aesthetic, apparently. It gives the guards more of an air—they want smart soldiers, they say, not nonentities.

To stand at ease, the position is: one foot forward, one foot back, head slightly inclined. Then on the command 'Atten . . .' you jerk your head back, but without moving the rest of you, and then when he says '. . . shun!' you give a little jump and bring the back foot forward with a bang, heels together and toes apart.

This drilling went on for forty days. We were also taught how to salute. They made us fit a stick of wood inside our caps to keep the points stiff and straight. To teach us the salute, the corporal went and stood in the middle of the square while we marched round him. Whenever you went past the corporal, you had to hold your left hand stiffly down your side and raise your right hand to your cap. Thumb and fingers straight and to-gether, hand pointing at the forehead, touching the cap above the right eye. Then the corporal would pretend to be an officer, and call out: 'You there, step forward!' and the man had to step forward smartly, and as soon as he came up to the corporal who was acting as officer he had to bring his feet together with a click, and stand smartly to attention and salute. After he had run up and saluted, he had to lower his hand and remain there at attention, chest out, eyes fixed on the officer's face. You're not supposed to move your eyes, even, because if you move your eyes you can't help moving your head too, and that's not allowed. If you move at all, you've had it. Goodness only knows why, but that's the rule.

Once I had to speak to the Captain. I went into the quarter-master's office—and there was the Captain. Well, I leapt to attention exactly as I'd been taught, and saluted. 'What do you want?' he says. I started to tell him—but what was I to do? You see, I wasn't allowed to move, yet I couldn't give him a proper answer without using my hands to show him what I meant! I couldn't explain just in words—every time I started talking, I couldn't help it, I started to illustrate with my hands too. How on earth are you supposed to talk to someone when you're standing there as stiff as a ramrod, and can only talk with your mouth, and not use your hands! 'Stand to attention!' the captain says: 'I haven't told you to stand easy, have I?' So I just shut my mouth and gave up trying. But after a minute he says: 'All right, stand easy,' and after that of course we were able to talk, since I was allowed to use my hands again!

Then they taught us 'eyes right' and 'eyes left'. When the company is formed up and you're all marching along, the officer calls out: 'Eyes . . .' and you jerk your head up, still marching along, and strike the ground firmly with your boots; and then when he says '. . . right!' you jerk your head round to the right and stamp your feet down on the ground, all in step. You have to go on marching with your head turned round to the right, or to the left as the case may be, until the order comes: 'Eyes . . . front!' On the word 'front', you jerk your head round to face forwards again, and give another stamp with your feet. This was how you saluted on the march when the troops were in column, they said—it was all part of the training drill. They taught us all this sort of stuff; and then they began training us to kill men.

We started off by throwing dummy hand-grenades, then eventually we went on to practise with live ones. The first time we had to do it with the live ones, I was dead scared. First a soldier came round handing out the grenades from the ammunition box, one to each man—just as if they were apples or something. Then we had to line up in fours on the range, behind gaps in the bank. You put your helmet on, and an officer came and stood beside you. 'Ready . . .' he said—and the first time, I flung the grenade over without waiting, the minute I'd pulled out the pin! It really put the wind up me—I'd never had anything to do with the beastly things before. But I soon got used to it, and by the end of course I didn't care a damn.

Then there was rifle practice. At the end of the range, they set up six wooden targets in the shape of men, for us to fire at, and you just had to hit the dummy for it to count as a man killed. If you got all six shots on target, you won a prize. Then there was the machine-gun: each soldier fired six bursts, about forty rounds in all, at the six dummies. If you missed every shot, the captain used to fly into a tremendous rage.

You should have seen the amount of ammunition we used up—whole lorry loads of it, disappearing just like that! We were gobbling up grenades. With these great heavy machine-guns, the ammunition boxes were emptied in a minute. Mortars by the dozen—heavy mortars and light. And the pistol practice, too. This was in the Infantry: as for the Artillery, every shot they fired meant thousands of lire down the drain—one thousand lire at a time! By this time, I'd been sent to join the regiment. This kind of training went on for eleven months; and then we went on manoeuvres.

We trained all day long, till five o'clock in the evening, and then we were free to go out on pass till nine. It was like a lot of birds being let out of a cage. Those four hours were all the free time we had. The officers used to lecture us about how we must behave ourselves outside barracks, how we mustn't make a nuisance of ourselves by pestering respectable girls . . .

Well, that's the life of a soldier in peacetime. If they'd at least taught me something useful—something about mechanics, say—well, that would have been all right. But all this 'quick march' and 'eyes right'—what the hell was the use of all that to me and my family?

What was my job before? Let's think now—I'd tried my hand at a lot of different things. At one time I used to go out gathering capers, and grasses for making brooms; I've been a plumber, a navvy, a confectioner, a frog-catcher, a snail-gatherer; I've collected wild pot-herbs and olives; I've been a gleaner of fallen olives and corn after harvest; I've collected scraps of charcoal in the woods, and bits and pieces of coal dropped along the railway lines, and lead from spent bullets on the *carabinieri* firing range; I've been a seller of second-hand American clothes; an ice-cream seller; a roasted nut and seed pedlar; a pedlar of water and anise; I've sold snails, and caught freshwater eels, and sold contraband American cigarettes, and contraband drink; I've sold old iron, too—I used to wrench the brakes off carts with a pair of pliers, and steal crosses out of the cemetery, to sell as old iron. Occasionally I managed to get a job as a labourer. But even that's not all—I'm sure there were other things, too, that I haven't mentioned.

For all those eleven months, I never sent a single lira home to my father: in fact, it was him who had to send money to me. It was just a useless waste of time. When I came home, I was quite out of practice with my work, I'd just about forgotten how to use my tools.

Nobody would go into the army of their own free will, except the ones who take it up as a career for the sake of the money. If a man can't think of anything else to do, he may either join the police or enlist in the army. He'll become a lance-corporal, then corporal, then sergeant, and earn his living that way. But as for doing it simply from choice—no one in his right mind wants to join the army and go to war. It's only because people don't know any better. If only everyone could get together, we could clap up the three or four madmen who do want war in a lunatic asylum, and let them fight it out among themselves!

I'll tell you my idea of what ought to be done instead of all this ridiculous military training: each year, they should send all the servicemen to work in a particular area—in Sicily, for instance. It would be the Government who'd pay them—and of course they'd also have to see to it that the rest of us weren't put out of work as a result. Then instead of all that money being wasted on armaments, it should be spent on the work these troops would do: reafforestation, making roads, setting up new industries, building government subsidised houses for the poor, building dams—everything that's needed here. They could do a year in Sicily, say, then a year in Sardinia, then a year in Calabria, and so on. Have you any idea how many thousands of men are called up for military service each year? After ten years of that, just think of the improvement—the whole country would be far better off. And of course you'd get people to do this kind of service much more willingly: 'Today I'm working for other people,' a bloke would say to himself, 'but tomorrow it'll be for my own family.' At the moment, we're all too ignorant and narrow-minded; but if only we could become a bit more open-minded, and if only we could unite, then we could surely get this done. After all, what could anyone do to us? They couldn't possibly arrest us all. They couldn't arrest the whole of Italy—how would they ever feed that many?

All these armaments are no use to anyone—we don't need them. We become fathers, and watch our sons grow up, and then when they get to twenty we have to see them go through the same stupid business all over again. Why can't we teach them something good instead? Why shouldn't we see them grow up to a proper, sensible life? This seems so obvious it stares you in the face. No one can say it's not true: ask the biggest idiot in the world and he'll tell you it's true. We should teach our children only good things, not bad, wasteful things like killing people. We should only kill for the sake of honour, or for matters of personal interest. I may not be an educated man, but I *know* this idea of mine is a sensible one.

I am practically illiterate, but I know there are quite enough conscripts in Italy for us to be able to make all this conscription useful to the community, instead of such a terrible waste of money. If you're a working man, you lose your job, and then you have to waste months and months on all this boring nonsense. Obviously you'd be happier doing something profitable, some useful work, or practical training of some sort. If the Government was to bring this in, would anyone have anything to say against it? Who could possibly object?

Anyway, what happened to me was that I was recalled for the war: four years of it, and even worse hell than before. After a seven or eight days' crossing on the *Liguria*, we landed at Tobruk. Even though I'd done my military service, I found I knew absolutely nothing about the front line—I tell you, I was completely lost! I'd only been there three days when the battle started, and Tobruk was bombed for the first time. Whole houses were blown into the air. With every raid, more houses were destroyed. Then I was sent to the front line.

Arms, legs, heads, boots with the feet still in them—it was chaos. People screaming. A bomb would come over and burst and blow up everything in sight. But I don't need to describe it—everyone knows what war's like. I thought of my family, and put my life in the hands of the Madonna, and we would look round at each other and try to raise each other's spirits a bit. But then when you see a man killed, when you see another friend die, you forget about everything else—even your wife and children. You're just not a human being any more.

# The 'healer' [1]

TO CHARM away worms, you must first treat your hand with a cardoon. They're a kind of wild artichoke, you find them in the countryside. It's at their roots the worms breed. You dig them out, and at Eastertide, on the afternoon of Good Friday when they're putting Our Lord on the cross, you rub the worms on your hands. You have to have three worms, because they nailed Him on the cross with three nails. You squash the worms, and rub them over your hand, and then for three days you mustn't use that hand at all, because you've got to keep the dead worms on it. Then you pass your hand over the belly of the person who has worms, and say the prayer.

If someone's in a bad way with the worms and needs treating quickly, then you can mix up a potion for them. Sometimes the worms give children fits. Their eyes go glazed and they froth at the mouth, and they either start to breathe heavily, or else they almost stop breathing altogether. When this happens at night, a child may die. Lots of them die that way. The worms crawl up into their throats and choke them. If a baby only forty days old gets the worms, how can it call out to its mother? It happened to one of my son's boys once—'Pepè's dying! Pepè's dying!' the others shouted, and he was crying out: 'Mamma! Mamma! They're eating me alive!' He's ten now, my grandson. His eyes were staring out of his head. Then there was the other one, Biagia's child: he died. Nobody knew why, until they saw the worms coming out of his nose.

When you feel the worms up your hole, you can pull them out with your fingers. Those worms are the harmful ones, they really bite. Some of them are short, about as long as your hand, but you get others as long as your arm. Sometimes a person may manage to pull out half the worm, but then it breaks,

[1] This speaker is a woman.

because it's quite soft, and so the other half is left inside. You can pull them up out of your mouth, too.

We're all full of worms, you know, every one of us. The worms toil away inside us, and naturally they have to eat. We've all got worms. We have to eat for them as well as for ourselves. Everybody's got worms, even though they may not know it. Everything we eat goes down to them, and the more we eat, the fatter they get. They eat, and work, and move around inside us—they wander about all over the place: up the middle, to the right, to the left, all over our guts, looking for something to eat. They never touch the liver or the lungs, though. We've got two bags inside us, and if the worms can't find anything to eat there, then they start biting and bothering us. If you were to go into a cemetery and look at a child that's just died, you'd see how many worms it's got—so many it would take you two whole days to count them. The lice come out on a dead body, too, and all sorts of other things go crawling about. When we die and stop eating, they get hungry, so they come out and start eating our flesh.

There are little worms and big worms: it all depends if a person has bad blood or not. If they have sweet blood, they'll have many more worms. Big ones, small ones, they all breed together and make more worms. There was a man here once had a tapeworm for seven years, and when it came out it was over four yards long. If you've got a tapeworm, however much you eat it's never enough.

If you put some of the little worms in water, you can see them squirming and wriggling about. They're white, those ones: you can hardly see the babies, though. Then there's the bigger kind, which are dark. And then there's the tapeworms, the worst kind of all. They can even kill a man. You can't get rid of this sort just by laying hands on the body—they get a grip with their teeth and hold on much too tight.

When I was seven years old, Father Gioacchino fell down in the road. No one went to help him up, so I went over to him, and I said: 'Hold on to me'—because he was an old man, you see. So he held on to me, and pulled himself up; and when he was standing up he joined my hands together, and made the sign of the Cross on my shoulders, and on my hands, and on my chin. Then he said: 'Serve the people,' and then he went on his way to Canicatti.

I wasn't yet thirteen when I treated my first patient. The little boy next door had broken his leg, and I seemed to hear a voice in my heart telling me to go and see him. So I slipped into the room along with all the others; and when I saw the bone sticking out and the flesh all torn, I at once started telling the doctor off. 'Don't you see, the bone's sticking out underneath?' I said. Then I took hold of the boy's leg, and stretched it, and reset the bone, and then I bound it all up. Within forty days, it had healed quite straight. And ever since that day, I've had every sort of person come to see me: they climb all the way up here to have me heal them—*carabinieri*, officers and NCO's, lawyers—all sorts. As for the country folk—goodness me, I get ten a day at the very least. On busy days you can't count them.

People are the same the world over: they're just the same here as anywhere else. When a man loses his temper, his blood boils up inside, and he gets all upset. Anger can bring all sorts of ills on a man, including worms. And it's just the same when someone gets a fright—their heart turns over inside them. Don't you get all wrought up when you're angry? We had a lawyer here once—he was our landlord, as a matter of fact—and he started to go a bit weak in the head because the worms got into his brain. He was all set to become a judge—but in the end he died. He died howling, like a dog on a chain—'Ow-owowowowow!' —because it hurt him so much. It was the worms, they'd got up into his brain.

Another time there was a lamb that went mad and started running about all over the place. They took it to the butcher, and he split its head open, and inside was a swarming mass of worms—it was the worms that had driven the poor creature mad. When someone goes mad, it's because the worms are eating his brain. If a man gets terribly worked up over something, it sets the worms going, and in the end he goes crazy. The nerves—and the worms: they bring a lot of ills on us. When your blood gets stirred up, lots of nasty things can happen. For instance, getting very angry can bring you out in boils. There's a man I know who faints every time his nerves get upset—he just passes clean out and falls down on the ground. Obviously he's got something inside him. And if you give a child a fright by whipping it, that can bring on the worms too.

We've all got worms, you see, but they only get stirred up if a person's upset, if they've had a shock or something. That stirs up the blood, and the worms get stirred up too, and that's what makes the person ill. When you see a dog coming at you, if you stand still, then the dog'll stand still too: but if you start to get angry with the dog, then the dog'll get angry too. Well, it's just the same with the worms: if you get angry, they get angry too, inside you.

Most of the time, the worms live in our guts, in the bag where our food goes: but sometimes they come up. When a baby's born, it gets its worms through its mother's milk. Worms are useful to us, of course—we couldn't manage without them. How else d'you think we keep alive? Who d'you think digests our food for us? Our food's got to be digested, hasn't it? If the pot's boiling, anything you put in it will cook —and so it is with the worms: they cook the food for us in our bellies. Every mouthful we take goes down our gullet and into the bag—we've got two bags, one for food and one for urine. When the stuff gets down into the food bag, then the worms eat it. That's what they're for: to digest our food for us. If a person didn't have worms, he wouldn't be able to digest his food, and he'd die. That's the way God made the world: without the worms, nothing else could live. If there's anything the worms can't digest, we get rid of it with castor oil.

There are plenty of us healers around here who treat people for worms, women and men. Twenty? I'd say there were more like fifty of us here in Palma di Montechiaro.

Another thing that's brought on by anger is trachoma: it's caused by a rush of blood to the head. If someone gets very angry, the blood rushes up from the body and bursts out in the eyeball. And a fit of anger can also make a woman miscarry. Anger's at the bottom of all our troubles.

To treat the eyes, you use water from a drinking-trough where there's green weed growing, or else you can rub the green weed itself into the eyes. That'll get rid of the pain and make the eyes better. The reason for its healing power is that cows and mules drink from the trough, and their saliva is good for the sight. Another way is to dissolve the saliva of a mule or a cow in water, and bathe the eyes with that. All illnesses come either from anger, or from what we eat. A really bad fit of anger can kill a man.

Once, my brother-in-law was sleeping out in the country-side, and he woke up and found himself all red and swollen, and he'd lost his voice too—he couldn't utter a sound. When he got back to his house he tried to call out to his wife to let him in, but of course he couldn't as he had no voice. So he knocked on the door instead—but his wife didn't realise it was him. 'Who's there?' she said—and there was no answer. He just went on knocking, and she was afraid to undo the bolt! He took quite a fever. After a bit, he felt an itching on his arm, and when he looked, he found a tick clinging to him.

The poisonous ticks are the ones we call '*cammarate*'. If you get one of these on you, it'll poison you. And you mustn't pull them off your skin: you have to cut them away with scissors, because if you try and pull them off they tear and leave the poison behind. But if you cut them, you can get the poison out too.

There are always ticks around, with all these animals living in the houses alongside the people. The ticks breed from the stench of the beasts. Animals' skins are full of worms—you should see how many worms there are on a goat. You just squeeze the flesh, and the worm'll come out like a piece of spaghetti. Sheep are the same. Ticks live on dogs and other animals, and as the animals sleep in the house alongside the people, the ticks pass on to us. There are several sorts. Some are fat and white, and then there are the coffee-coloured sort which cling on with their feet. They poison your blood.

Then there are lice. Two things cause lice: dirt, and over-excitement. There are three different kinds of lice. First, there's the head-lice, the ones which live in your scalp: they come from over-working the brain. Say you've got a bill to pay, or some-thing—well, you get all worked up worrying about how you're going to pay it, and that brings out the lice. That's why we poor folk always have more lice—we have more worries, like how we're going to feed our families, and so on. The worries go round and round in your head, and in the end they turn into lice, and come out and start feeding on your scalp. Now, I worry about how I'm going to pay my rent. We can't really tell why they come, but we know they do!

Then there are the body-lice, crabs. Everyone has those. You may not think you've got them, but you have, even if you haven't noticed them. They live off our blood. When they start biting, it itches so much that you scratch and scratch, you just can't stop scratching. This sort comes out of the ground. I caught mine that way.

Then there's another kind which live on animals and chickens, and human beings can catch those, too.

I'll tell you an excellent remedy for wounds: urine, mixed with Streptosil powder and sloughed-off snake skins.

# What is waste? Salvatore answers

WASTE? If things are wasted here? Well, what exactly d'you mean by wasted? By *sprecate* do you mean *spigate*? *Spigate* is what we call plants that grow in a spike.[1]

By *sprecate,* d'you mean when things go bad? Well then, yes, there is waste. Say a plant of broccoli goes rotten, or an orange falls off the tree—Portugal oranges, we call this sort here—if one of them falls off, well then, that's waste, because we can't sell them. If they've fallen on the ground, that's that—they're spoilt, and no one'll buy them.

Or suppose I go out into the fields to milk the cows, and the calf comes up and wants to suck from its mother too, and it gets excited and starts pushing in—over goes the pail, and all the milk spills out on the ground. Well, you can't get that back, so that's waste too.

Then there's the peaches in summer. The fruit sets well, and starts growing nicely, but then you get this bug that eats its way into them and makes them fall off the tree. That means they're wasted, too.

Another thing: if an animal gets ill and dies, the carcass has to be burnt, as the meat won't be fit to eat.

And tomatoes often get diseases, too: black rot, ash blight, oil blight . . . or else they may be attacked by ants. Then if any fruit does set, it just goes rotten and falls off. So you see, plants can get diseases and go to waste, just like animals, and even us humans, too, when we fall ill.

No, there's no other sort of waste in the countryside.

Water? Yes, I suppose water causes waste, too, in a way: it spreads dangerous diseases to human beings and animals, because it carries sand which gives you diseases like kidney

[1] He is confusing two words: *sprecate* (wasted) and *spigate* (spiked, in the botanical sense).

trouble, and stones in the liver. And of course illness means waste. A lot of money is wasted on illness.

Then there's the fruit that has worms in it, for instance. You just have to chuck that away, you can't sell it.

No, there's no other kind of waste.[1]

No. I've never really thought about it, you know. But I suppose when something goes bad after a year's work, it must be meant as a punishment.

Working in the fields year in year out ruins our clothes, too, and when they get too ragged to go on wearing, we just throw them away.

Does our family ever discuss ways of making a better living? Yes, we do. You make more money buying and selling than you do just toiling away in the fields all day. It doesn't matter what you buy and sell—fruit, or greenstuff, or snails—anything'll do, so long as you can keep a roof over your head.

But there's waste in that, too. Suppose you buy some fruit, and then you don't manage to sell it. After you've had it on your hands for four or five days, you just have to throw it away. Now, there's waste for you! And it's the same with any sort of stuff you can't sell.

So now I've told you all you need to know about agriculture and trade, because I'm well up in both these arts. I've told you all the answers.

[1] For an account of the appalling waste of natural resources (and of human life) in Western Sicily, see Dolci's book *Waste*.

# Miraglia, a victim of the Mafia

## HIS STORY TOLD BY A FRIEND

I FIRST met Miraglia when he was about fourteen or fifteen. I used to see him often at the place that used to be the tailors' workshop. I don't know whether it was just because he was friendly with the man who owned the shop, or whether he was working there. Anyway, he was certainly studying to be an accountant even then. I knew he was studying accountancy. Then for a long time he was away from Sciacca, and I didn't see him at all. They said he'd gone to Milan, and then to France. When I saw him again he was twenty-two or twenty-three, and working as an accountant for the firm of Gallo and Company, brick manufacturers. After that, he became manager of the Rossi Theatre, which was eventually demolished, and then he had various other jobs before he finally settled down here on the coast in the fish curing business.

In 1944, as soon as the fighting was over, they opened the local Camera del Lavoro[1]—there hadn't ever been one here before—and he became its first secretary. His job was to recruit members, and issue membership cards, and to organise a party which would fight for justice and the rights of man. He told them: 'If you'll all get together, and organise, and form co-operatives, then through them we'll be able to get land for you all.' Everyone agreed, and in one year we'd recruited 800 members. But we didn't get any land after all, as there weren't any more fiefs to be broken up: the rich were allowed to keep two hundred hectares each, and so there was still no land for us.

No one had ever explained things to us like this before—no one had ever come forward like this. There'd been other parties before—Bertolino's party, Friscia's party, Murnuna's,

[1] A left-wing Union, most of whose members would be poor country people.

138

and so on—but they'd always been standing for Parliament, or for Mayor. Miraglia was quite different: what he wanted was for the people to unite and claim their rights, which they had always been denied. He said that with proper organisation our Party could come to power.

My ideas weren't all that different from his, but still I wasn't a Party member. Then one day when I was in his house he asked me if I'd take out a membership card, and I agreed. 'Tell me,' he said, 'wouldn't you like to join the Party? What do you think of this organisation we're building up now?'

'It's probably the only thing to do,' I answered, 'though I've never seen anything like this in my life before. Still, I can't help thinking it's bound to lead to trouble. Let's face it, this Government has enormous power, and it certainly won't be easy to chuck it out at the elections.' From what I'd seen in the past, I was of the opinion—and I still am—that this Government would not give way. They've been in power so many years now that they'd do anything, absolutely anything, rather than lose—even down to killing us first. I was thinking of Panepinto, you see. I remembered the time he came down here, with Verro, to a meeting of the Farmers' and Farm Labourers' League. That was around 1909. And before long they'd killed both of them, first Panepinto, then Verro.

'But times have changed,' Miraglia argued: 'We don't have to deal with a Monarchy any more'—because at that time, you see, there was a left-wing Government, with Togliatti as Minister of Justice and Gullo as Minister of Agriculture.

He was absolutely devoted to the poor, Miraglia was: his one idea was to help them, and he really fought for it. Before the war, he used to go about on his own most of the time. He wasn't the sort to hang around all day in bars. You would see him walking about by himself, with that little goatee beard of his—he looked so odd with that funny little beard. In winter, he used to wear a round fur cap with ear-flaps that buttoned up on top: he looked just like a Turk or something. But in fact he was a really good man. A really good, decent, kind-hearted man. With that long overcoat he used to wear, you might have thought he looked a suspicious character, specially with that little beard which gave him such a foreign look. Whereas really he was so kind and friendly and well-spoken: not at all the sort you would expect someone to shoot down in the street one day—you'd never have thought it.

Miraglia was never one to waste words: he'd say what he had to say, and then shut up. He wasn't at all the sort who goes around chatting and gossiping everywhere, and making all sorts of empty promises—not at all. And another most unusual thing about him: he would always be the first to greet someone in the street. That used to amaze me. If he knew the person's name, he'd say: 'Good morning, so and so,' and if he didn't, it didn't matter: he'd still say 'good morning' as he passed. The people were mad about him—it was as if the sun had come out and was shining on them at last! He made it seem as though we practically had everything within our grasp already—but unfortunately, of course, it takes time. They've never fogotten him in Sciacca, they still think of him.

All this time, he was working at the fish curing station, down by the shore. He used to go down to work there early in the morning, and then at half past eleven he'd come up to the Camera del Lavoro. That was how his day went.

He took a very long view of things, and had grand ideas for the future. He knew that one day the world must change, and he worked towards that goal. He came of a poor family himself—he had his roots in the soil. He was always very careful and exact about everything, and never neglected anything. Whatever he started, he'd be sure to finish it; and he never put his hand to anything without first thinking it over and working it all out beforehand. When he was arrested by the Fascists in Mussolini's time, the people thought to themselves: 'The Government have arrested him because they're afraid of him.'

He spoke beautifully—he was very well educated, very precise and exact in his language. He really knew how to put his experience into words, and how to express his strongest feelings. The one subject that really made him fierce was the question of helping the poor: otherwise he was mild and gentle.

That's the sort of man he was. And he would never dream of pushing himself forward, or trying to set himself above ordinary people. He'd queue up along with the rest, if need be. One day he went to the fishmongers and found several other people there ahead of him, and so he went and took his place at the back of the queue. After a while along came a priest, a certain Padre Arena, and when *he* saw the queue he went straight into the shop and up to the front, and bought his fish. When he came out again, he said to Miraglia: 'Look, I've got my fish already —and you're still waiting at the back of the queue!' And Miraglia answered: 'I may be at the back, but I'm not as backward as you'—meaning that the priest was uncivilised. But all the same, they respected each other, those two.

Whenever there was a problem to be solved. Miraglia would at once call on whoever was best qualified to advise on it. I remember once I was sent for because he wanted to find out which of the Agricultural School's houses were within the Abbey boundaries, since those houses would belong to the Abbey. He always took notes. And he was a real thinker, too, always working things out in his head. He was always taking notes: the minute you started to talk to him, out came his notebook, and he would jot things down and then tuck the notes away in his bag.

Well, he came in for some fierce criticism. His enemies went round saying that he was just taking us all for a ride. He was asking the impossible, they said: he was stirring up the people to take the land away from the rich but really, they said, we hadn't a hope of succeeding. They mocked him, and kept up a continuous campaign of gossip against him. And to think that the rich got the land in the first place for practically nothing, because the people were too afraid of being excommunicated! I know that's what happened—I had it from my father.

He really knew how to draw the people round him, Miraglia did: they flocked in, like birds to a bait! He had only to say: 'Meet you here tomorrow morning'—and the place would be full to bursting. Everyone came. Some of us understood what he was talking about because we knew it from our own experience, and the rest managed to understand just because he was so kind and careful and patient at explaining. Even when he was working, if anyone went to see him he would at once stop whatever he was doing and go and help the man, no matter who he was.

When he was Chairman of the hospital board, it was his business to arrange the contract with the goatherd who supplied the milk for the hospital patients. One day when the contract was nearly expired the goatherd went up to Miraglia's house to ask if it could be renewed—and Miraglia at once made out a new contract, without question. This made a real impression on the goatherd—it seemed such an unusually kind thing for any-one to do. So d'you know what he did? He brought Miraglia a present of a cheese weighing about sixteen or seventeen pounds! 'Look,' he said, 'I've brought you this cheese—it's only a small present, but I hope you'll accept it in return for the favour you did me.'

'But it wasn't a favour,' Miraglia answered. 'You mustn't bring me presents like this! You've got me wrong if you think I do anything for what I can get out of it. We shouldn't do favours for what we can get in return—either a thing is just, or it isn't; and if it is, then we do it because it's right, and not for any other reason.'

He couldn't bear to think of the poor being looked down upon. 'I'll help you as far as I can,' he used to say, 'but it's up to you to organise yourselves. You must get organised.'

None of his helpers worked for money: each one willingly did his bit for nothing. When the Statute of the Co-operative was drawn up, I was called in because of my previous experience of co-operatives. I was the oldest in the group, and had the necessary practical knowledge: so the Statute was drawn up according to what I thought would work best. It was to be a limited liability company, in which everyone would answer for his own share, rather than a collective co-operative. The Board of Directors and the Chairman were all to give their time free. Miraglia wanted it to be called 'La Madre Terra'—'Mother Earth', which was a much better name than any of the other co-operatives had: they were called things like 'The Most Holy Annunciation' or 'The Ex-Servicemen's Co-operative', or 'The League'. Meetings were to be held once a fortnight, and we were to work Sundays for no pay. A man would only get paid if he lost a day's work through having to go out to clear up some trouble or other in the countryside, or that sort of thing.

Miraglia arranged all this voluntary work. 'We must each make our sacrifices for the good of the organisation,' he used to say. He knew that the work of the Co-operative, and the organisation in general, would take up a lot of his time, and so he always used to get up very early in the morning. He was always stressing the need for organisation, and he used to go round organising meetings, group by group. On Sundays, he would work till one o'clock in the afternoon, and then go home for lunch; but by four o'clock he'd be back again, and then he'd stay on till nine at night. The people began to learn—they really did begin to learn things!—because he always explained everything so clearly. 'If we are organised,' he used to say, 'we are all one brotherhood. If anything goes wrong, then we get together and discuss it.' He used to urge the people to come together in a brotherly spirit. What he wanted was an organised brotherhood, in which everyone would nevertheless enjoy his own rights: he'd been an Anarchist, you see. But of course the people weren't used to this way of seeing things. Their attitude had always been: 'I'm not going—you go.' They were used to quarrelling amongst themselves: 'What are you doing here?' they would ask each other suspiciously. You see, they were so used to being tricked and done down. But he was trying to get rid of all this suspicion and malice.

As the people got to know him in this way, he became enormously popular. If ever he hadn't any work on down at the harbour, he'd always be out among the people. There was very little work to be had in those days. All the master-masons were unemployed, and they used to spend a lot of their time with him. Berto was one of them, and Triolo. And Turi Citrolo was always there with him, too: he'd been there right from the start, as Treasurer, and Miraglia always kept an eye on him to see that he didn't make any mistakes in the accounts—he was new to book-keeping, and Miraglia wanted to make sure the accounts were properly kept and up to date.

On summer evenings, they used to walk down with him to the salting station where the fish was cured. 'Man ought to be perfect,' Miraglia would say. 'A man should try to understand everything, know everything: he should be capable of understanding anything.' It really upset him to see so many people unable to write even their own names—the number of illiterates here is fantastic. But even if the people didn't really understand what he meant by being perfect, they were still touched by his words. They hadn't the education to know quite what perfection meant, but they liked his talk all the same—and in any case, they got some idea of what he meant just from the example he set, and they were encouraged to try and follow his example. If ever any of them failed to understand something he'd been saying, he would patiently repeat his explanation all over again.

The first demonstration we had, Miraglia rode on a white horse. (Afterwards, the man who'd lent him the horse got into hot water with the other side—they were angry with him for lending it!) On the Saturday evening, we decided we would organise a cavalcade through the town so that everyone could see how many people were behind Miraglia in wanting land. So, next day, all the country folk and the farm labourers gathered together at the prearranged time.

I'd had to go out into the countryside myself that morning, so that by the time the procession came along I still wasn't ready. My house is on the corner here, and so when the procession, with Miraglia riding at the head of it, came up that street and turned into this one, there he was in full view of my window. I would have drawn back, but it was too late—I didn't want to hurt his feelings even more. But as soon as he saw me, he smiled; and though he bit his finger at me as much as to say: 'So you've let me down'—he was only joking. I could tell by his smile he forgave me, because of my age—I was sixty-seven then.

Behind him came all the people: they'd ridden into Sciacca from all over the place—Menfi, Montevago, Santa Margherita, Sambuca, Burgio, Caltabellotta, Lucca, Ribera, Calamonaci and Villafranca. They were all laughing and gay. Some of them shouted and whistled whenever they came across any supporters of the other party. (But none of the rich appeared on their balconies that day!) Lots of the men had their sons riding up in front of them.

And Miraglia, leading the cavalcade on his white horse like that—you might have taken him for Roland himself! He was a lovely man, he had such a presence, and he made such a fine figure on a horse. It was a joy to see him. The little children threw flowers at him. And there behind him came all the people . . . Yet these people were the very same ones that drew back in fear, after the first wave of indignation, when he was killed: the very same people who, seeing what had happened, tried to conceal the fact that they'd ever belonged to our Party. So that only the very boldest among us stayed on, only those of us who were really committed to the movement, and were determined to stay at our posts even in the face of threats, to do or die.

It was a long cavalcade. By the time the end of the procession reached my door, the head of it must have already passed San Michele. It seemed to go on for ever, even though they were riding in two columns. From San Michele they went on down to Porta Palermo, and then they came to a halt in front of the Town Hall. The police had come into action by this time, and were doing their best to break up the demonstration. There were four or five thousand mules, and dozens of bicycles as well. Sympathisers all along the way were waving and clapping enthusiastically, and the womenfolk lined the route waiting to see their sons or husbands who were riding with the procession. When they reached the sports ground, they stopped, and Miraglia made a short speech to explain why they had held the cavalcade. He was very pleased with the turn-out, and thanked

K

his various helpers, and also thanked all the people for coming. And then he sent everyone home.

It was from that moment onwards that his enemies really began to hate him, because they saw he was winning the entire town over to his side. But this demonstration also succeeded in impressing the Commission on Uncultivated Land, so that as a result the redistribution of land did take a spurt forward too.

The first land to be taken over was the Santa Maria fief. Two or three estate agents had control of it at the time; and it was decided to occupy the land, turn them off it, and then divide it up into smallholdings—all of this being in accordance with the new law on uncultivated land. (At the present time, that whole fief is divided up into smallholdings.) Cavalcades like this had already been held at the time of the Sicilian Fasces. Miraglia suggested to the Co-operative that we should take possession of the fief—it was his idea, and he undertook to lead the people. 'But how are we to go about it?' he asked: 'How are we going to get everyone there in the first place?' Most of the people who wanted to go and claim the land were day-labourers and didn't have horses, so they would have had to get there on foot, unless they had bicycles. But they joined forces with the peasant farmers who had mules or carts or wagons, and in the end almost everyone managed to get hold of some sort of mount, or find a place in a cart. The rest went on bicycles.

Again Miraglia rode at the head of the cavalcade, this time on a piebald horse, dappled black and white. What with all the day-labourers, and all the smallholders from around Sciacca, there were more than fifteen hundred people in all. Everyone was jubilant at the idea of taking possession of the land. Of course no harm of any sort was ever intended: but so few of these people had any clear idea of what was happening, and of course hardly any of them realised that if the holdings were too small there'd be no profit in them at all. It seemed enough to them just to get a bit of land of their own—that gave them courage, and made them feel stronger: and so that led to other cavalcades.

Miraglia's aim was to raise the standard of living of the poor people. And as that couldn't be done without taking something from somebody else, somebody was bound to lose by it. After the fight over the Santa Maria land, he launched into another battle—and of course this made his enemies hate him all the more. What was this new battle? Well, it was over the tenants' rents, the thirty per cent business, and over the profit-sharing agreements between landowners and *mezzadri*—he wanted to make sure the *mezzadri* got their lawful sixty per cent. Of course that made his enemies really detest him, and that was when they started to prepare the noose for him. That was the beginning of the end. It was then that they started to make up to him. Why else do you think they should have made up to him so much in the last few months of his life? I'll swear they were trying to get in with him then so that if anything was to happen they could claim to be his friends and so wouldn't be blamed. They'd started plotting it already.

At a meeting in the Town Hall one day, he told us that he'd been warned to withdraw and put an end to these activities. Up till then, he'd always refused to carry a revolver—he was always opposed to murder and violence of any sort. But after he'd been threatened, he took to carrying a revolver round with him all the time, either in his bag or in his belt.

I know the sort of thing they'd have said to him: 'Look,' they'd have said: 'why not give up all this silly business? Just think of what might happen to you. As it is, you're quite well-off, and you've no need to stir up all this trouble. Besides, think of your family . . .' and so on. We used to see one or two nasty looking faces at most of our meetings, right up to the night of the murder. If he'd been able to denounce immediately, in public, the people who'd threatened him, things would have been different. But they were too canny: they did it in a round-about sort of way. They didn't say anything openly to his face, and so he could never be quite sure whether he really was being threatened or not. Surely they couldn't really have been threatening to kill him, he would think to himself . . . I know just how they go about it, because I was threatened once myself. They took me aside and said: 'Listen, you're an old man now—why should you want to go and get mixed up with all this? Don't you think you'd be better off just staying at home?' —all very smooth, you see—'You don't want to get mixed up in politics: you leave that to the politicians—you don't want to lower yourself to their level!'

Well, this is how the murder happened: he must have been betrayed by some false friend, someone who'd been pretending to be a Communist but was really in league with the Mafia. It happened on the 4th of January. It was a nasty night, that night—the *tramontana* was blowing down from the north off the mountains, and it was very cold. When the meeting at the Camera del Lavoro was over, they walked up via Roma, and then two of the Comrades went on with him nearly as far as his house. When they got to the lampost there, he stopped them and told them to go back—he didn't want them to accompany him any further. 'You go off home now,' he said: 'it's too cold.' Besides, it was only a step to his house now, and there was no sign of anybody round—they were hiding, of course. So the other two turned back, and he went on up to his door. He was just fitting his key in the lock when they let fly at him with the tommy-gun. The first round missed him—you can see that from the bullet marks in the wall. But the second burst got him in the neck, and he fell there in front of the door. The minute they'd got him, they fled. Two of them rushed up the hill towards Santa Caterina, which was the quickest place to hide—they were terrified of being seen, of course.

In Sciacca, it was as if the end of the world had come. Everyone was shocked, and terrified out of their wits. Enormous crowds gathered in the town, and he was given a splendid funeral. Even the rich joined in the funeral procession. They knew what was good for them!

Normally in cases like this the Police do their best to hush everything up. It's regular policy, the order comes from the Ministry of Justice itself. It's always like that—I've seen it happen so often. But in this case, the Superintendent had had quite a bit to do with Miraglia, so that they'd actually become quite friendly—that is, as far as it's possible for anyone to get friendly with the police, and specially considering the situation in 1947. So that, for once, they did make some arrests. One of the men they arrested was so terrified when they caught him that he messed his pants and had to change his underclothes!

Everyone was expecting something to be done. It was said that the murderers had confessed everything, right down to the smallest detail, and a statement was even issued from police headquarters in Agrigento. And then they were all released—they were supposed to have been found 'not guilty'. Later they were arrested again, but again they were let out, apparently because they'd found an alibi. At least, that was the story.

After that, instead of getting promotion, Superintendent Zingone and several others were transferred: obviously some-one wanted them out of the way. So the reactionaries had won. Over and over again it happens like this, whenever big issues are at stake. And not only that—the officers weren't just removed: they were charged with having used torture to extract the confessions. The preliminary investigations by the Examin-ing Magistrates were pure formalities. And besides, these investigations are always secret, so no one ever hears the result and the proceedings are never published. It's all done on the quiet. They're cunning, these people, and they get good lawyers.

Eventually, the police officers were cleared of the charge of torture. But in that case, if they *hadn't* used torture, then it surely follows that the confessions must have been true after all. However—might is right. Whenever things take a dangerous turn, they deliberately try and muddle everything—it's like a pot of water when it comes to the boil: the water gets all churned up, the water from the top goes to the bottom, and the water from the bottom comes up to the top, so you just don't know where you are any more. They just try and make the whole issue thoroughly confused. Even though there was an obvious contradiction somewhere, they just let the whole thing drop.

Of course, if it had been a rich man who'd been killed, they'd have found the murderers soon enough. But in a case like this they take advantage of their position to do what they like. Last year, forty or fifty smallholders in the country around Sciacca had their chickens stolen: fifteen, twenty, thirty birds at a time. (Not to mention all the cows and mules and sheep that get stolen all the time—there's not a single farm that hasn't had some of its stock pinched.) Anyway, not a trace was ever found of the thieves. Then one night some thieves broke into the estate of one of the rich landowners. They climbed over the boundary wall and got into the enclosure; and when the owner's alsatian wouldn't stop barking, they shot it. The watchman didn't stir—he was much too scared. Next day, the landowner reported the theft to the police, and of course they took the matter up at once, and set up road blocks on all the roads which the thieves might possibly use. Before very long, they stopped an *Apa* truck (it's called the *Apa*—'bee', because the motor-bike is called the *Vespa*—'wasp'), and inside the truck they found a whole lot of chickens—which in fact had been stolen from somebody else! So you see, as soon as the interests of the rich are at stake—hey presto! and there is an *Apa*, complete with chickens and thieves. It's always the same, in everything. We've seen it happen so often.

I'm an old man now, and it's always been the same, ever since I can remember. Over and over again, whenever there's been a murder by the Mafia. In this district alone, they've been responsible for the disappearance of Montalbano's son and for the murder of Spagnolo of the Camera del Lavoro. But even on the Government side, they disagree so much amongst themselves that they're always having each other killed: there was the lawyer Campo, for instance. And Leonardo Renda—he was shot and stabbed, and then the murderers left a stone in his mouth as much as to say he should have kept his tongue from wagging. It's a little trick the Mafia have—they like to leave a message of that sort as a warning to others. Like when they shoot a man through the mouth, meaning that he shouldn't have talked so much. Then there was Almerigo, the Mayor of Camporeale; and Giglio, Mayor of Alessandria della Rocca; and Vito Montaperto, Mayor of Campobello di Licata—and that's only mentioning a few from this province alone. There have been so many you couldn't count them all. Their way is always to shoot the leaders, in the hope of frightening the rest into staying quietly at home. And of course the culprit is never found. The verdict is always: 'Murder by some person or persons unknown'—and there the matter rests.

And so it was with Miraglia. That's how things stand now, just as if nothing had ever happened. Nobody does anything about it. What are we to think? Might is right . . . They are more powerful, so they can twist and suppress things just as they please, while we're left to look on helplessly.

Everyone was scared. When the men came out of prison again the second time, the whole business was dropped, and no one ever really knew what had happened. Then, very gradually, people began coming back to us—some of them are only just making up their minds to come back even now. But of course the minute the Mafia go and commit another political murder, our supporters will all be off again in a panic. After Miraglia's death, his enemies began to come out into the open; they felt strong enough to act as they pleased. They took courage, and even looked forward to seeing the Camera del Lavoro in the hands of the Christian Democrats.

If you want something, you've really got to fight for it, otherwise you'll never get anywhere. Because we've never been united in claiming our rights, we've always been despised, ill-treated, robbed, killed. That's been my experience all my life through—it's always been the same old tragedy. And the rich are canny: they see to it that we keep fighting amongst ourselves, and destroying and killing each other, in the struggle for land.

None of the co-operatives we've formed have been proper collective co-operatives—their aim has been simply the re-distribution of land. It's quite useless trying to form proper collectives as long as people are so mistrustful of each other. The only sort of co-operatives that can succeed here are the sort where everyone gets his own piece of land and works it himself. Miraglia suggested that the whole fief should be worked collectively, and the profits divided among all the members—but they weren't having that. On that point, they wouldn't even listen to him, so he had to give up that idea. For that to succeed, the first essential is for the people to have faith in each other, and that's just what they haven't got. And no wonder, since they've never had justice themselves.

At present, we're not having any more cavalcades. What's wanted here is the will to unite and claim our rights and get rid of all this crowd who are battening on us poor people. We must make ourselves into a disciplined organisation, and claim our right to justice, and our right to work.

When you have work, you can come home in the evening and sit down with your family and eat your plate of soup in peace, in the sure knowledge that you'll still have your job tomorrow. When a man has a job, he feels secure, he has peace of mind—he doesn't have to keep house with despair. Once you know for certain where your daily bread's coming from, then you're able to build up a family.

I spent three years in America, and there I used to work all week, from Monday through till midday Saturday. Then on Sunday I used to take a trip with the family into the countryside. We used to go out to Cento Appacche, and walk in the woods there, and listen to the music: and we used to pick wild herbs there just for the pleasure of it—because we liked doing it, not because otherwise we'd die of hunger, like here. That's a better life, over there.

Everything I've told you is true, because I've seen it all with my own eyes. It was going to America, and seeing what went on there, that taught me all I know. I was twenty-four when I went, and up till then I hadn't known anything at all about life, as I'd always lived an isolated life out in the countryside. Then when I came back from America, I began to realise the need for a government which would look after the poor and see that there was work for everyone. And ever since then, I've always stood up for the underdog.

# Antonio, a fisherman

WHEN the fish see the lamplight, they come darting up, almost jumping out of the water; then when they come to the surface they stop there, all packed together with their noses pointing straight upwards, as quiet and tame as a flock of sheep. They come to enjoy the warmth, you see; they like it under the lamp, just the same as we like crowding round the stove in winter. They can't get under the lamp fast enough—they zip along, jumping to get there more quickly, leaping out of the water as if they were flying. And then they all crowd together underneath the lamp, rows and rows of them, all standing upright, with their mouths opening and shutting, opening and shutting.

But let me tell you what's happening to the fish nowadays. Take Sciacca, for instance. Here, there are about a hundred engine powered fishing boats, each one taking about sixteen to eighteen men on board. They go out every evening, and along with each motor boat there'll be two or three rowing boats with lamps. There's always a great bustle on board—shifting boxes, seeing to the fuel, fixing up the acetylene lamps, stuffing the bombs with clay and stones so that they'll sink at once . . . I'll tell you how these bombs are made: you take two sticks of explosive from the pack of thirty, and you stuff them into a tin, packing them well down and making sure the fuse is all right. Then on top of the explosive you put a bit of oil-paper, and on top of that you stuff in a lump of clay—that's to stop the water getting at the explosive. Then on top of that you put in some stones, and you pack them round with more clay: that's to make sure the bomb will go straight to the bottom. Each of the motor fishing-boats will take about a hundred of these bombs when they go out in the evening. They have to carry a lot, just in case, because they never know how the fishing's going to go—which direction they'll have to take, or where the fish'll be, or even whether they'll find any fish at all. Of course the blokes who aren't so well off can't afford to take so many: the stuff costs 4,500 lire a pack.

Well, when evening comes they put out to sea; and when a boat gets to a suitable stretch of water, it drops anchor and waits till the fish begin to gather. On a good night, you can see the fish all seething round, great shoals of them; sometimes they're so densely packed together that they seem like sand. When you reckon you've got about ten or fifteen quintals there, then you chuck in the bomb. After the explosion, you see all this great mass of fish floating to the surface: hundreds of them dying, with their backs broken, and hundreds more completely stunned and drunk-looking. The ones nearest the explosion are killed outright. Masses of them are blown to bits and just get washed away by the currents. And of course all the small fry in the shoal for yards and yards around are killed at once and washed away.

Always they kill many, many more than what they catch. And what's worse is that it's always the young ones that are killed off first, so that means all those fish completely lost. It would be the same, for instance, if you were to chuck a bomb in here, wouldn't it? Some of the adults might survive, but all the little ones would certainly be killed. Well, just think now: if you have a hundred of these motor fishing-boats going out, and each one of them destroys, at the very least, twenty or thirty quintals of fish every night—well, just work it out for yourself! There are times when one boat alone may kill several hundred quintals of fish in one night.

When we throw this explosive into the sea—(yes, I mean 'we': I go out myself from time to time along with the worst of them!)—when we use this explosive, the sea gets all messed up around the boats, and the fish won't come under the lamp any more. It gets all stirred up and murky—all the mud comes up from the bottom. When you chuck the bomb in, you can watch the fuse as it plummets down to the bottom leaving a trail behind it—it goes on burning, you know, even under water. Then when it blows up it goes: 'aaoof!' That's the noise it makes—it's not like an ordinary explosion. 'Aaoof!' From a distance, it sounds like a proper bang, but from close to all you hear is this 'aaoof!' and then the water splits apart. The force of the bomb exploding flings up water and mud and all sorts of stuff from the sea bed, and all the fish burst out of the water and then fall back again. Then as the water gradually begins to clear again, you begin to make out all this great mess of fish, heaps of them being swept away by the current, all mashed up, their backs broken, and the big ones just drifting about completely stunned and stupefied, and with their backs all dislocated. Yet as long as they've a little bit of life left in them, they still struggle to stay near the lamp. Even when they're at their last gasp, they still try and drag themselves up to the light—and they go like this with their mouths, look . . . That's how they want to die, under the lamp. They love the lamp. They can see perfectly well in the dark of course—it's just that they like the lamp-light better. When it's dark, the fish all get into a close shoal: you see, it's their nature to go about together, these fish. And perhaps they're more frightened when it's dark, too. Even if I bang on the side of the boat like this, they still don't go away, they like the light so much. It's only natural: it would be just the same with a man, wouldn't it?—if he was stunned and his back was broken, he'd rather stay in the light too, wouldn't he?

Anyway, the next thing is to throw over the nets and catch them. The dead ones and the stunned ones are no use—and there are hundreds of these, whichever way you look: underneath the boat, to right, and left, and on every side, nothing but dead and dying fish. Fifty yards away and more you can still see dead fish, and then they're carried away by the current. We're not moving ourselves, of course—the boats are anchored, at twenty fathoms.

All through the night the boats are coming and going—some in one direction and some in another, some just setting out while others are going back to harbour. From the shore you can hear the 'aaoof!' of all the motor-boats flinging in their bombs, all night long.

When it's right under your boat, you hear 'chaoof!' and

sometimes it feels as though the boat's splitting apart, as if some great fish was heaving up against it—just as if a huge fish was bursting up through the boat. You see something like a wild beast leaping out of the darkness, and some sort of white thing seems to be dragging at the boat: a dead fish, it looks like, or a dog, or a man, even—goodness knows what—and it drags along with its mouth open. Here at Selinunte a shark pulled Russo Francesco off the boat one night, and then it took a hold of the boat itself. Afterwards, you could see its teeth still stuck in the wood, one whole tooth and a whole lot of broken ones. It must have weighed about six or seven quintals, that brute.

Sometimes we throw these bombs to drive off the dolphins, because if they see all the fish crowding in they'll come leaping into the net after them and rip it all to pieces and gobble up the fish. So we fling a bomb to drive them off—but we send it over the top of the water, so that it explodes in the air. It makes a terrific bang, enough to deafen the whole bay, and that scares off the dolphins. They're no good to eat, dolphins: their flesh is the same as human flesh. What are we made of? Blood, and very little flesh—there's not much to us. And if you get a dolphin and slit it up like this with a knife, it'll all drain away in blood. It'll give off over two gallons of blood. And we're the same. Blood, and oil: very little flesh. But fish are quite different, now: they're solid fish, and they hardly bleed at all.

A hundred engine-powered fishing-boats, and three hundred small craft—unless it's a full moon, of course. Each motor-boat might use something like twenty bombs in a night: six bombs to each lamp, say; and since each motor-boat is usually accompanied by three rowing-boats with a lamp each, then that comes to eighteen, right? And that's only a rough average—often they use far more.

One night, over by Terrasini, a man was blown up, and all his sons with him: every one of them died. And at Mazzara, one man had a bomb explode in his hand, and his whole hand was blown right off: all he had left was a stump like that.

All the newly hatched fish are killed by these bombs, every

single one—there's not a hope of any surviving. Even the tiny little fish inside the eggs. All the small fry are killed, always, and even the spawn is wasted. Us men with the little boats don't do too well. After a motor-boat has chucked in a bomb, all the other fish around dive straight to the bottom in fright, and after that it'll be about half an hour or three quarters of an hour before they start to come up again to the lamp. Then if they throw another bomb in, the fish all shoot off down to the bottom again. And so we can't get much fishing done. Of course officially it's forbidden to use the bombs. The penalty is having our boats confiscated. From time to time the authorities come down on us for an inspection—but it's always the little boats they search: they never bother to set foot on board the motor-boats. Of course the big shots who own the motor-boats have some arrangement with them!

Sometimes, you may find yourself in a patch of calm water where there's no current at all, so that instead of being washed away all the little dead fish are left in the net. You just have to chuck them back in the sea—they're no use to anyone, you can't sell them. You go and scoop them out with your hands, and they're all gluey—they just turn to slime in your fingers.

I know all the fishing grounds round Terrasini, and Trappeto, and Castellammare too. Over that way, they don't use bombs— or anyway only a few. Over there, it's not the bombs that are destroying the sea like around here. They'll maybe use a bomb or two if they see, say, a quintal of *ope* (that's a little fish, about this size, which is eaten all over Italy). But they don't use them much. It's not the bombs that are the menace there: it's these motor powered boats from Palermo that come over to fish for the *spogliata* with the kind of net known as a *raustina*. This net has such a close mesh that it hardly even lets the water through —it's almost like cloth. The mother *spogliata* (they're called *spogliate*[1] because when they're very young they're quite naked, as smooth as a needle, with no scales at all)—anyway, the female fish produces all these baby ones, and they're all caught and killed too, even the tiniest. So that all these thousands of young

[1] Naked.

ones will never even have a chance to grow up—just think what a loss that means! All those fish wasted, killed off like that when they're tiny. And by now, of course, there aren't many fish left at all. The fishing grounds are just being ruined. And there's all the little prawns and shrimps and things, too. Wherever this dense net passes, it destroys everything—it's like when they burn the fields: fire on this side, fire on that side, so which way are the poor creatures to turn? Naturally the fish don't like this bit of sea any more, since even the little shrimps and things they live off are disappearing; so the ones that escape the nets go right away and try and find some other stretch of water where they can feed properly again and lay their eggs in peace.

Here at Marinella there are about sixty boats. I know the whole coast around here, all the way up to Mazzara, Marsala, Trapani. There's an awful lot of fish destroyed up that way too. They use potassium compound around there. The worst place of all for that is Mazzara. They chuck out the nets and circle round like this, and then they throw in the potassium; and that means that none of the fish within the circle of the net can escape, upwards or downwards, so they're all caught. Then for months afterwards, not a fish will come near the place because of the stink. It smells foul even to us, but to the fish it's terrible—it's like a poison gas to them. If I was to throw a bit of this ash here, we wouldn't be able to smell it at all. But that other stuff is a kind of spot-remover, for taking dirty marks out of clothes, and it really stinks. It's deadly to the fish. Where it's been used, you won't see another fish for months and months. It takes a good many storms to wash away the smell.

So: first they let down the net; next, they scatter this potassium stuff on the water—it comes in chips, little pieces like this, hardly bigger than those tablets you take for headaches. Then they wait for a few minutes while the stuff dissolves, and soon the sea around turns quite white, because it works like lime. It makes the fishes' eyes go all red and bloodshot, and blinds them, so they can't see which way to swim out of the net. With the bombs, the fish'll come back to the same spot after two or three days—but with this stain remover, it'll be months and months, and specially in calm weather. I'd only have to use that stuff once in these waters here and the whole village would be starved out. They do this first in one place, and then in another —and of course wherever they do it all the small fry are destroyed as well.

From Partinico to Castelvetrano it's only seventy-five miles by land, but by sea it's a hundred and twenty-five: a hundred and twenty-five miles of confusion and chaos. To see the fleet from the shore at night, you'd think how lovely and festive it looks, with all those little lights, like a town all lit up for some celebration. You people looking out to sea think: how pretty! But really it's all one horrible confusion. Not at all the beautiful festival at sea that you might take it for, but a vicious cut-throat struggle, where one man throws a bomb and the rest are put out of their living. And all those fish being slaughtered, fish with their backs smashed, hundreds and thousands of quintals of fish lost, wasted: a fortune being destroyed at sea. In the old days, hundreds of little boats used to come here from all the coast around, to fish in the bay off Selinunte. But today there are hundreds of fishermen out of work, because these fishing grounds are ruined.

# Santuzza, a gleaner

I CAN'T go gleaning any more, because I haven't any spectacles. There's no work I can do now, because I can't see at all from a distance, and only very little close to. I used to go gleaning every year after harvest, searching all the fields in the country round about here. I used to start out at three in the morning, or two, even, because the earlier I set out, the more I'd be able to gather. I used to get dreadful backache, bent double like that all day long, but at least I managed to collect a bit of corn to eat. How would I ever have managed in winter if I hadn't had that little bit of corn put by?

I've been a widow twenty-four years now. I've had my bad years, when there wasn't much corn to be found: but there were good years, too, when I would find plenty. When the corn ears were nice and fat, I might take home a good eighteen pounds of grain: but in a bad year when the ears were lean, it might only be about twelve pounds, or less. When I got home, we used to thresh it with a bit of wood to separate the grain from the husks, and then we winnowed it by tossing it up in the palms of our hands so that the wind blew away the chaff. Then we shook it in a sieve to get rid of all the dirt, till at last only the grain was left, all lovely and clean.

I tried again this year, but I couldn't find anything. I went out every day for four days, but I couldn't see any corn at all, and so I came home empty-handed. I could just see the stubble, and when I bent right down to see if there were any ears of corn left, a bit of stubble spiked me in the eye. That was six months ago, and my eye still hasn't got better. It's like having a black eye—it's as if I'd been punched. Since then, I haven't been able to recognise people from any distance at all. I keep wanting to rub my eyes, I'm always taking my hanky to them and rubbing away at them like this, to try and get them clear, but it makes no difference. It's as if there was a mist in front of them all the time.

If you haven't any money at all, all you can do is to shut your-self away indoors and just sit there all day. If only I could go gleaning again and get a bit of corn to sell, I could buy a pair of spectacles with the money, and then I'd be able to see, and so I could work again. I used to manage to glean for nearly a month —mostly corn, it was, but other things as well. Tomatoes, for instance, the little dry pear-shaped ones. And other work, too, I used to do. If only I could still work, I could make some money and buy myself some spectacles, and then I'd be able to go on working again. But without spectacles it's hopeless, I can't do anything. They tell me that if I wore spectacles for a bit my eyes would be rested and I'd get my sight back.

Around here, we're all hard up, so who can I turn to for help? My married daughter would give me the money if she had it. Her husband has had to go to France, now, because he couldn't find any work here. She'd give it me if she could—but in any case, how could I ever ask her for it? If she was still single, well . . . but now that she's married, how could I? The poor girl's never had enough herself, let alone any to spare to help me.

Have I asked who? The priest? But what has this sort of thing got to do with him?

The Assistance Board? What's the Assistance Board? I don't know what that is.

The Mayor? Once when I needed money to buy medicine, he told me he hadn't any.

And it would come to such a lot, too. First, there's the oculist himself, and then there's the spectacles to pay for. And to get them I'd have to go all the way to Palermo, and that would mean eight hundred lire for the bus fare if I went by myself, and sixteen hundred if my daughter came with me. And on top of that there'd be the cost of the spectacles, and I don't know how much they'd come to. I've never had any myself. They tell me they cost ten thousand lire. Someone who had a cataract got a pair, and they had to pay eight thousand lire for them, or ten thousand, maybe—I'm not sure. I'm all muddled now.

But when I have something to eat, my sight seems to improve a bit, it gets a little clearer, and then I feel more cheerful.

L

# *A journey*

EARLY one morning when it was still quite dark, Bruna,
Libera, Cielo, Ruggero, Amico and I set off from Partinico to
walk all the way over the mountains to Palermo.

After we had gone a few miles, Libera observed that if she
looked down at her feet as she walked, the earth seemed to be
rushing away beneath her, and yet in the distance it seemed to
be standing still—it *seemed* to be. Then someone suggested that
we should try making a poem together, and I agreed to join in
too; and in the end not one but four poems were composed
(at least, for us they were poems), before we came out at last
on Bellolampo and looked down on Palermo, clear and beautiful
in its wide bay.

## I

When you look down at the earth beneath you
When you are walking
It whirls away giddily under your feet.
But if you look some way ahead
It comes more slowly towards you,
And the further you look, the stiller it seems.
Firm in the flow of the ages,
Blue under the wheeling stars.
The earth seems still.

## II

Even smoke can be beautiful too,
Rising from burning weeds,

Or from the chalk pits
Or from some chimney in winter
As we saw at Borgetto,
Gently rising into the thinning mist,
Into the clean sky.

### III

Up in the open above Montelepre
Eating our fresh-baked bread and cheese
Looking down over the wide bay
Cielo flings sharp blue rockets into the valley.
Now we are walking through white fields scented with
   honey.
'What shall we call this walk today,
All the way to Palermo?' asks Libera.
'A walk' says Danilo.
'A journey' says Cielo.
'Then what would it be if I went to India?'
'A journey' they say.
'Then what should we call our walk today?'
'An excursion' says Libera.
'And in fifty years time if you go to the moon?'
'A journey' they say.
'And in fifty years time if you go to India?'
'Just an excursion.'
'In a hundred years time . . .'

### IV

Walking, walking . . .
'What do you think poetry is?' asks Danilo.
*Bruna:* 'It's verses.'
'So if there aren't verses, then it's not poetry?'

'It's something that comes from your mind and your heart.'
Cielo says: 'Poetry's looking at mountains,
And the sea and the earth and trees and plants,
And getting to know the whole world,
And then writing it down,
And then starting again to try and learn something else.'
'It's something so subtle,' says Bruna,
'That there's no other way of expressing it.'
'Poetry's this,' says Cielo: 'when you really understand it,
Then everything seems better,
And it makes a person happier.'
As we round the curve of the mountain road
A placard comes into view.
'If I see on that placard the name "LEACRIL"
Is that a poem?'
*Cielo:* 'No, it's a poster.'
*Libera:* 'But you could make poetry even out of a poster.'
*Cielo:* 'But there's nothing beautiful in an advertisement,
    is there?'
*Libera:* 'You can make poetry out of any word, anything.'
*Bruna:* 'But it must be a thing that already has poetry in it.'
*Cielo:* 'Poetry's not just a matter of, say, ending the line
    with an "m" '
*Amico:* 'Poetry and music say things that can't be said just
    with words.'
'But what *is* poetry?'
'I know what it is,' says Ruggero:
'You must think of something quite new,
Something that doesn't exist yet.'
'So poetry's like a journey, then, always going further
    and further.'
*Cielo:* 'Icarus was poetry at first—
The dream of being able to fly.
But now there are aeroplanes, so it's not a dream any more.'
*Ruggero:* 'Flying can still be a dream, for someone who's
    never done it.'
*Cielo:* 'So flying can still be poetry.'

*Libera:* 'And for a bird, too, flying is still poetry.'
*Bruna:* 'If the bird feels like we do this morning,
Going on its way, journeying, discovering new things.'
*Danilo:* 'So you think, then, that poetry's a journey, always
    going further and further—
And also a way of seeing better a thing that is near and
    familiar?'

# *White horses*

THIS TIME, Daniela (aged four) and Chiara (aged six) are also with us.

| | |
|---|---|
| *Amico* | White horses are always the fastest runners. |
| *Daniela* | Yes, white horses are more beautiful, and they're stronger, too. |
| *Cielo* | Because they're lighter. |
| *Daniela* | Yes, they're lighter. |
| *Chiara* | Yes, of course the white ones are lighter. |
| *Danilo* | Why are the white ones lighter? |
| *Cielo* | Because they're happier. |
| *Amico* | They're lighter because the white is paler, and so it's lighter. For instance, when I'm wearing white, I can run faster. |
| *Chiara* | The white is lighter. |
| *Libera* | But there are some white horses that are not so strong, and some dark ones that are stronger. At last year's August races, I remember, there were three horses: one dark brown and two light brown—and it was the dark horse that won. |
| *Cielo* | Ah, but the two that lost weren't *white* horses, were they! |
| *Danilo* | Chiara and Amico, what do you say? |
| *Chiara* | I'll have to think first. |
| *Amico* | Well, if we go by what Libera just told us, then it's the dark ones that are fastest. |
| *Cielo* | But if the two paler ones had been *white* horses, they could have won. |
| *Libera* | But what if the white horses were tired, and couldn't manage to overtake the dark one? |
| *Cielo* | Well, perhaps the dark one might be in better **training** |

than the white ones—or perhaps it might be the other way round.

Then I suppose that would mean that running faster and winning depends on training more than on the colour of the horse.

*Libera*   Yes, that's just what I was getting at.

*Amico*   Now I come to think of it, I agree with Libera and Cielo—I think they must be right. If a horse is tired or weak, how can it run well?

*Cielo*   Perhaps the two paler horses ran less fast because their shoes hadn't been put on properly, and a nail had come loose, or something. Or maybe they were smaller, and took shorter strides.

*Ruggero*   It depends on the jockeys, too.

*Danilo*   Well then, what does the greater speed of a horse depend on?

*Chiara*   How d'you mean?

*Libera*   He means, what makes one horse run faster.

*Amico*   I'm not a specialist in horses, so I couldn't say which sort are fastest. To find out for certain, I'd like to try out a whole lot, and make them run one by one, and see which was fastest.

*Cielo*   It depends on their training, it depends on their strength, and on the length of their legs. And on their age, too.

*Chiara*   Yes, when a horse is old it's not quite so strong.

*Danilo*   And does it depend on the colour, too, if a horse is faster or slower?

*Daniela*   White horses are faster—I like them best.

*Chiara*   A white horse is faster when it's well trained, and when its legs are longer, and when it's stronger.

*Libera*   Could you repeat the question you asked just then?

*Danilo*   Does it depend on the colour as well, if a horse is faster or slower?

*Libera*   The thing is, we like white horses best, and so we *want* them to be stronger and faster than other horses. But in order to be certain that what we *want* to be true really *is* true, we'd have to test it out, like Amico said.

*Cielo*     Yes—for instance, we like to think that trees talk to each other—that even trees are alive too. We like to think that all sorts of things do really talk to each other; even though we can't hear them, we like to think they do talk all the same. But we'd have to test it out to see if it was really true.

*Libera*    And also, we would like it if the stars talked to each other: but we'd have to try and test if it was true. It must be true in a way, though, because we know they attract each other, and so there must be some sort of communication between them.

*Bruna*     And another example. People say that all men are brothers, because they'd *like* that to be true: but we only have to look around and see how the Mafia oppresses the peasants, and how no one does anything to find work for all the unemployed, and how people won't get together and co-operate but go round shooting each other instead, and making war. For men to be brothers really, they'd have to unite and co-operate—whereas now it's still 'every man for himself'.

*Cielo*     You know when we went on the Peace March the other day? You remember the policemen marching along on our left, every ten yards or so? Well, why didn't the one beside us answer when I asked him what his name was? And then when Amico said 'Perhaps he's dumb'—I still don't see why he gave us such a nasty look.

# *For the young*

To RETURN to my opening theme:

Only fifty years ago a dictionary could still define *politics* as 'the art and science of proper government; astuteness; use of cunning and deception in order to advance oneself'. Today, what we must understand by politics is the complex of activity by means of which people and countries determine the direction of their lives: politics must become both a personal and a collective instrument for social progress. Instead of the art of government by a few men invested from above with the power to command, politics must become a complex instrument for determining correct courses of action, an instrument for acquiring the precise knowledge necessary as a basis for action, and the means by which individuals and peoples can develop their own character through the exercise of personal responsibility.

Though group life and political activity have of course always had a certain educational value, clearly in the past the group would have been regarded more as a means of exercising power than as a means of acquiring the knowledge and understanding necessary for fruitful action.

Perhaps it would be useful here to contrast some of the characteristics of the old style of politician with those of the new—and by 'old' I mean outmoded, out of date: I do not mean old and new in a chronological sense, because obviously there were 'new' politicians centuries ago, whereas today there are still all too many 'old' ones.

| *The 'old' politician* | *The 'new' politician* |
|---|---|
| Commands and imposes | Directs by identifying himself and developing with the group |
| Centralizes power | Stimulates and co-ordinates a variety of groups and personalities |

| *The 'old' politician* | *The 'new' politician* |
|---|---|
| Secretive | Communicative |
| Rhetorical | Simple and to the point |
| Corruptor | Educator |
| Violent | Non-violent |
| Tends to join the side most likely to win | Tends to take the side of the weak and oppressed |
| Opportunist: changes tack according to more or less immediate advantage | Sets his course according to his conscience—though continuing, with his own and other groups, to test the validity of his attitudes |
| Intervenes with negative sanctions to block progress | Joins in to try to encourage new research |
| Uses intelligence, knowledge and technical skills to impose himself on others | Uses intelligence, knowledge and technical skills to try and get the best out of himself and others |
| Expert in double dealing and intrigue; if loyal to anyone only to his own closed group | Direct, sincere and open with everybody |
| Has the qualities (adapted and refined to suit the time and place) of the man of war | Above all constructive |
| Enjoys and exploits his power: essentially an exploiter | Works responsibly for others; essentially an improver |
| Cultivates a clientele | Stimulates and co-ordinates democratic groups |
| Upholds and defends old structures | Creates new structures |
| Delegates power according to personal relationships | Delegates power to whoever is most capable |
| Public actions determined by need to reinforce his own power | Stimulates plans for development making the best possible use of everybody |

There is an obvious spiral here: a political system which considers and values the individual and the group will create a better and more healthy society. And, conversely, higher economic and cultural standards, a more effective use of group relationships, and a fuller symbiosis between individuals and the community, mean a more advanced political system.

Vast numbers of people, hundreds and hundreds of millions, are today still unable to have any say at all in fundamental decisions affecting the whole world. By seeking to bring about changes which would enable all those at present excluded to participate, we would also help to create a situation in which explosive conflicts, harmful to all, would be avoided. However, the vast numbers of people today excluded from decision-making (and this not only in underdeveloped rural areas but also in industrial zones, even in the heart of great industrial cities) cannot just sit and wait for the opportunity to participate to be handed to them: it is not going to come from heaven. It is no use expecting those who are at present enjoying and violently misusing power to be suddenly and spontaneously willing to share this power with others in order to transform the world. We must realize clearly that the creation of a new world is something we must struggle for—it can only be the fruit of hard work, care, sacrifice, wise organisation, constant pressure—and patience: we must not expect to achieve *the* revolution, *every* revolution, the *whole* revolution, in three days.

All over the world, under the most diverse systems, because of the insensibility and lack of foresight of reactionaries problems are aggravated to the point where they are bound to explode into violence: yet the explosion is also partly the fault of the excluded who—ineffective, or resigned, or frightened—allow the contradictions to continue and the old ways to be consolidated.

Reform is difficult to achieve, because the new is not easily understood. And the more genuinely revolutionary any new proposal is, the less acceptable it will be to whoever stands to lose by it—to the powerful and the privileged. In order to have genuine revolution, we must have genuine participation by those who are at present excluded and deprived; and we must always bear in mind, too, that whereas progressives are on the whole motivated by a general good will, conservatives and reactionaries tend to be driven more by immediate self-interest, so that even though they may be less worthy and less intelligent than progressives, it often happens that they are more efficient and successful—(by which I mean, of course, successful in attaining their own personal ends.)

It is of fundamental importance, then, that in all conditions and at every level new forms of non-mercenary work should be promoted—whether it be with government support or in defiance of government—which will intimately correlate socio-economic development with active non-violence. Projects initiated quietly, humbly, to deal with particular problems, if tenaciously applied and pursued can eventually come to have an entirely new political weight, and bring about serious structural changes.

Taking stock of oneself, one's own problems, and one's conscience; comprehensive development; democratic planning; pressure for non-violent revolution: all these are indispensible, and essentially inter-related. Thousands of schemes have been initiated over the last few years in every part of the world—but all too often they work from the 'top' downwards, with the idea of help, of contact, of witness, of mere technical aid and so on, instead of promoting and encouraging self-analysis and the study of the most effective and economical forms of action, and getting everyone to co-operate in a common pursuit of progress. By now it ought to be absolutely obvious that what the deprived need rather than gifts is the possibility of under-taking and constructing the necessary alternatives for them-selves.

Today, total world military expenditure (and that is by no means the only form of waste and suicide!) amounts to more than one hundred and fifty thousand million dollars, or about fifty thousand million pounds: it is obvious what an enormous reconversion, what enormous reforms are necessary to break the bad habits of the institutionalised old world.

But the intuitive feeling for the need to create a new, non-violent world is spreading all the time. Whereas twenty years ago, or even fifteen, or indeed in many places only ten years ago, the conscientious objector, the person committed to new, non-violent methods, was commonly regarded as an out-of-this-world idealist, today the idea is so widespread that there is even the risk of its becoming merely fashionable, imitative, and ceasing to be a genuine commitment. The condemnation of force and violence is spreading all over the world. And just as old forms of settling issues, such as the duel, now seem absurd, so today young people find the question, for instance, of whether violence is committed according to the old norms of international law, according to the rules of the old game, an inadequate criterion for judgement. Even the traditional institutions seem to be aware of the need to bring themselves up to date: co-existence has become an ideology, and even in the Papal Encyclical *Populorum Progressio* there has clearly been an effort to modernise both language and content. Young people (who often seem to turn to non-violence almost instinctively) are coming to realise more and more that the traditional centres of religious and political power function rather as diffusers of propaganda than as centres for research, discovery and initiative; and, furthermore, that the political and propagandist pre-occupations of these centres mean that any seed of the new thinking that they may adopt tends inevitably to be corrupted. For example, when the idea of organic planning can no longer be ignored, all kinds of things are smuggled in under the label of 'democratic planning', all sorts of programmes in which the ultimate control is still in the hands of the old closed power groups. Or another example: a law is at last proposed which will recognise the right to perform an alternative, non-military national service—but only for graduates, i.e. only for the sons of the more prosperous classes.

More and more people are realising that just as we have to allow for, say, the physical law of inertia, so we must recognise that intelligence and technical ability generally lead to power, and power in turn tends to lead to the abuse of power, conservatism, exclusion. More and more people are realising that in so far as advanced technological development does not pursue genuine human ends, it creates nothing but an inflated farraginous emptiness.

Wherever nuclear weapons are being produced, wherever people are most aware of the risk of unleashing blind senseless violence, more and more young people are coming to reject violence altogether. And on the other hand the person who, out of a need to be 'realistic', to 'face the facts', seeks to overcome the old monsters by means of guerilla warfare is generally the product of a more technologically backward environment.

But all the time violence continues to explode, massive, murderous, ever more and more dangerous. How far is the healthy rejection of the doctrine that 'might is right' going to spread? To what extent are we constructing a practical, organic alternative to that chaos of misunderstanding, hypocrisy and betrayal, of unresolved problems exploding, of mad destruction, of consciencelessness and cunning, despair and exaltation, terror and hate, of the will to survive and of suicide (all presented, for the most part, under the guise of peace), that is war?

We have now reached a critical point when it is absolutely essential for us to realise that in the face of the possibility of total extermination we must, in order to survive, adopt the morality (both at a personal and at a political level) of non-violence. We have reached the critical point where—since pragmatism is no longer enough, any more than it is enough just to have vague intuitions, however worthy—as well as developing and co-ordinating practical protest and demonstration, we have also got to find the means of giving a concrete form to the new, positive way of life: new forces must be educated in the techniques of non-violent revolutionary development; the sociology of conflict must be studied; proper sociological methods must be applied in planning; experimental groups must be formed and co-ordinated—new, robust groups which will seek to make the best possible use of all resources, and which will take the place of the present system of clientship and patronage whether at a primitive level

or on a national or indeed an international scale. We must develop our own laboratories and workshops, so to speak, as positive and effective counterparts to the laboratories and instruments of dehumanised technology. We must not be wasted.

And so I come to the end of this long letter. I shall be most interested to know what your reactions are.

Yours,

Danilo

Partinico, Summer 1967.